Flavours a anecdote, from The Olive Tree Kitchen

£1

Mary Bouas

Dedication

I would like to dedicate this book to my mum, a fantastic chef and an amazing person who taught me everything I know about cooking.

She worked with us for more than 8 years, sharing and teaching me all the kitchen secrets and tricks she knew, and also passing on the family recipes she had learnt from her mum and the ones she created or perfected for herself in over 40 years of her journey into cooking.

I also dedicate this to Diana who has and will always play the biggest part in my life.

Thanks

I would like to thank Diana and Jeff. If it wasn't for the pair of them, this book would never exist.

Jeff for his patience, enthusiasm, brilliant photo skills, his love of food, and the endless hours, evenings and weekends he spent putting this book together. Thank you for coming out to Zakynthos and sharing some great time with us, cooking and tasting all those dishes, joining me fishing in my kayak, all the barbecues the laughter and jokes. My thanks to Jacquie too...behind every great man is a very patient woman. Now you can get used to eating a meal without waiting for Jeff to photograph it first.

I would also like to thank from the bottom of my heart all our amazing family, friends and repeat customers for sharing some incredible stories and supporting The Olive Tree for more than 30 years. You are my inspiration.

Diana was there for me from day one, she supported me all the way, sharing her ideas, correcting my grammar and polishing the book.

The two of us gave birth to The Olive Tree taverna back in 1984 and it's been our life ever since. It's time to share the recipes for some of those dishes that have meant so much over the years. Enjoy trying these recipes for yourselves.

...And don't forget, put some love in your pot.

Lakis x

Contents

TAVERNAS are usually handed down from father to son or mother to daughter and stay in the family for many generations. But for Lakis Bouas realising the dream of running his own taverna was not as straightforward.

To begin to understand why and how he came to own the most popular taverna in the bustling Zakynthian resort of Tsilivi, you only have to look at his lineage.

His paternal grandfather, Michalis, was a fisherman in Garitsa, Corfu, his maternal grandfather, Panayiotis, was a butcher in the suburb of Pyrgos, near Olympia, in the Peloponnese. His mother, Mary, was a chef and his father, Spiros, had a lifetime of experience of running kafeneion and tavernas. The love of food, it seems, is in his genes.

Spiros Bouas and Mary Kresteniti met in their mid-20s, while they worked in Athens. He worked for a company producing catering equipment and she worked in a firm which made batteries. Their paths crossed at the factory gates as Mary finished her shift and Spiros was about to start his. Flirting was soon followed by courtship and ended with marriage in 1960.

Lakis came into the world on August 23, 1962, as their first child, while they lived in the Athens' suburb of Zografou. A brother, Vangelis, arrived 18 months later in February, 1964, and the Bouas family was complete.

Life under the junta government became increasingly difficult for the population of Athens and in 1970, Spiros decided enough was enough and returned to his beloved Corfu with his young family.

After running kafeneion and tavernas with increasing success in Athens, ever the

Lakis and Diana in the summer of 1984

entrepreneur, he opened the Paradisos (Paradise) Taverna, near Corfu Football Club's ground in the suburb of Garitsa. Mary agreed to take care of the kitchen, Spiros sang and played guitar, the boys were the waiters and the Paradisos became a successful part of local history.

In 1974 things looked bad for Greece when Turkey threw a spanner in the works by invading Cyprus and the dark clouds of war threatened to engulf the country.

In 1980 Spiros became restless and seized the opportunity to run a bar-restaurant, The Aventura at Agios Yannis, near Benitses, half-way through the tourist season with the hope of securing a contract for the following year.

It was perfect and Spiros thought he'd found his idea of paradise. Sadly his plans were curtailed by an invasion of a different kind – the owner's son returned from a broken

up papers and had to report to Athens for his National Service and this effectively brought Spiros' latest taverna venture to another untimely end.

With Lakis based in Athens, Diana relocated to be closer to him, swiftly followed by Spiros and Mary.

Diana had no trouble finding work and, when Lakis had finished his service, they would work the winters in Athens doing any job available and spent their summers in Corfu, doing what they do best – hospitality and food.

The summer of 1983 found Lakis and Diana working back in Corfu at the resort of Acharavi, while Mary found a six-week seasonal job as a chef at a fish taverna in the sleepy little Zakynthian beachside village of Tsilivi.

Lakis spent the best part of the summer of 1981 trying to woo the new waitress, but with little success…

That short summer job of Mary's proved instrumental in Lakis' move toward fulfilling a dream of owning his own taverna.

Inspired by his mother's positive accounts of the island, he and Diana visited in January, 1984, and by the spring of that year had found the ideal location in which to start making that dream come true.

marriage in the United States and the hopes of a contract turned to dust...paradise lost again.

Undeterred, he opened another taverna, this time about three or four kilometres from the nearest resort of Benitses.

It was May, 1981 and it was at this point Diana arrived on the scene, working for Spiros as a waitress. Lakis spent the best part of that summer trying to woo her, but with little success. In September he eventually succeeded and they have been inseparable ever since. In October Lakis received his call-

Tourism in Zakynthos was in its infancy, but with Lakis' knowledge of the business, coupled with the stunning natural beauty of the beach and village, it was a foregone conclusion that the only way this could possibly go was up.

Tour operators discovered Tsilivi a couple of years later and the rest is history.

The Olive Tree started life as a little cocktail/snack bar, but it wasn't very long before the tourists were wanting more than toasted sandwiches and Lakis began to expand his kitchen and menu to satisfy his customers' needs. As Tsilivi grew in to a full-blown resort the little snack bar kept pace with demand and became a hugely successful taverna in its own right, and one which people return to year after year.

In 1991 Lakis and Diana welcomed their son Alexandros into the world. The family continued to live above 'the shop' in their tiny rented room until, three years later, they were able to finally move into their own home in the nearby village of Kypseli, where they have lived ever since.

In 2007 Lakis and Diana diversified with a new venture, building four holiday villas with a swimming pool on a piece of land they'd bought in their village some years earlier. Echoing their success with the taverna, they built this new venture up slowly but surely and it's gone from strength to strength.

Diana divides her time between running these and working in the taverna, which leaves Lakis free to devote his total energies to the passion which drives him...the kitchen.

When the tourist season is over they put both businesses to bed for the winter, harvest their olives, make their oil and finally find themselves with the luxury of a little time on their hands.

They relax by getting together with family and friends and enjoying lunches and dinners with them to catch up. Chat is punctuated with laughter at these gatherings with food still playing a starring role.

At Easter Lakis roasts a whole lamb on a manual spit, which means everyone takes their turn. 'If you don't take a turn, you don't get any lamb', it is said. I'm not sure if that would actually be the case, but I doubt if anyone would put the threat to the test. The smell of roasting lamb would be too irresistible, I'm sure.

Converstation at these gatherings is, of

Lakis at play...still cooking, this time its spit

course, interspersed with stories, most of them hilarious, some surprising and some sad, but each one adds a new paragraph to the verbal scrapbook of their life together.

Some of them go back to Lakis' childhood on Corfu when he worked waiting tables in a garden restaurant, while his mother cooked and his father entertained.

One story Lakis tells is of one night when he was run off his feet with a busy service.

He began to wonder what he had been doing wrong as none of the customers were leaving tips. The answer became obvious when he went back to the garden, only to see a pair of legs disappearing up a tree in the corner of the garden.

His little brother had been hiding there all evening, clambering down to collect the tips when Lakis was out of sight, then scrambling back up again and waiting for the next lot.

Another story tells of a summer's night in the restaurant where Lakis and Diana first met and worked together in 1981.

roast lamb for Easter and a brief break for a photograph

One of the regular local customers was Spiros, the taxi driver. His party piece was to lift a heavy wooden table aloft using just his teeth and dance around with it held high, to lots of applause from the tourists and whoops of 'Opa!' from the Greeks. Apparently he was convinced that this was the best way to impress the ladies and would challenge the male tourists to have a go for themselves. Of course, it isn't about strength at all, but about balance and shifting the weight to the right place, making it look as though you have an incredibly powerful neck and jaw - as well as impossibly strong teeth. Many customers would try and, understandably, all of them failed.

Until one night. A gentleman, having studied Spiros' performances on a number of evenings, stepped forward to take up the challenge. He made a valiant attempt to recreate the technique he'd observed, almost faltered, but brute strength and determination carried him through and he eventually held the table aloft for a few seconds to rapturous applause from the tourists and a look of disbelief from Spiros.

His glory was, however, short-lived when, as he lowered the table to the floor and walked away, his false teeth remained firmly clamped to the edge of the table.

There are just too many tales to mention here. You can imagine after so many years of being with people and sharing their holidays as they relax and enjoy themselves, the story count continues to grow.

Over the years many customers have become true friends. Year after year their customer base grows either by word of mouth or just by someone who drops in for dinner and enjoys not only the food, but the ambience of The Olive Tree.

Passionate about promoting Greek cuisine and hospitality, Lakis and Diana are happiest when they are doing what they love best – preparing and cooking traditional dishes and making sure that customers leave contented and happy and hopefully, as friends.

Oven temperatures

	Centigrade	Fahrenheit	Gas mark
cool	40-150	275-300	1-2
moderate	160-180	325-350	3-4
moderately hot	190-200	375-400	5-6
hot	220-230	425-450	7-8
very hot	240	475	9

In Greek cooking we're pretty relaxed about measuring ingredients, for example, if a recipe says three tablespoons of olive oil it doesn't matter if its two-and-a-half or four. A cup, for example, is any medium-sized mug in your cupboard.

Garlic and onion quantities can also be adjusted to suit your taste, the same goes for herbs. A little more or less is fine.

In my taverna we make sauces and stocks from scratch, but in my house as in every other Greek house it's simpler and quicker to use different flavour stock cubes from the supermarket.

Pepper and spices in general are better and tastier if you grind them fresh, but if you use ones already ground, its not the end of the world. Just buy little and often.

In Greece one of the most popular cheeses we use in cooking is kefalotiri. If you can't get it, a good pecorino or parmesan would do just as well.

Above all, remember this, the magical ingredients for cooking are, put on your favourite music, get yourself a glass of something nice and put lots of love in your pot.

Kali orexi,

Lakis

Picture by Laura Tams

From top, left to right: Diana bought two raffle tickets and won two groupers; The Olive Tree garden in 1984; Diana and Lakis; Lakis and Diana with waiter Nik in 1987. Second row from left, Diana and Alexandros; the original steps of the Olive Tree in 1985; Tsilivi High Street, 1985; Don, Pat and Ouzo Denis; from left bottom row:, Martin, Lakis, his dad Spiros and uncle Andreas; a postcard of Tsilivi in 1988; Lakis, centre, with Spiros Margaris, left, and Spiros Augoustis

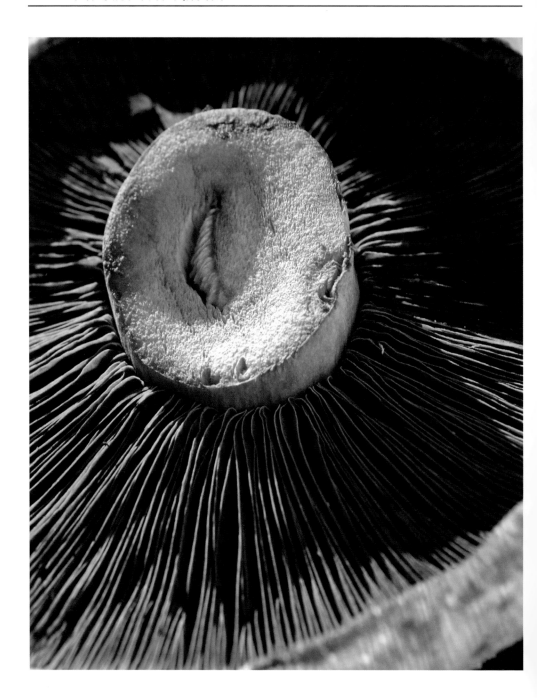

Soup

Soupes

This is a wonderfully warming winter soup, not one that I have at the taverna, but a favourite at home. The fresh chestnut season here in Greece only lasts a couple of months and this is a great way to do something different with them other than roasting them over the coals... which we also do a lot.

serves 4

2 leeks, cut into thin rings
2 carrots, cut into thin rings
1 celery stalk, cut into thin rings
1 onion, finely chopped
2 bay leaves
half a teaspoon of ground nutmeg
300g chestnuts, boiled, peeled and chopped
salt and pepper
3 tablespoons of olive oil
2 litres of hot vegetable or chicken stock

Heat the olive oil in a saucepan and gently simmer the onions for 1 minute.

Add the celery, carrots, leek and bay leaves and continue simmering for another 5 minutes.

Add the chopped chestnuts, stir, and then pour in the hot stock. Put the lid on the pan and leave to simmer for half an hour. The vegetables should be soft and the soup should be thick. If it becomes too thick during cooking, simply add a little hot water or stock to thin out as required.

Finally, taste and season to your liking with the salt and pepper.

*Y*ou can make this lovely smooth soup at any time
of the year, but it's perfect for my taverna menu
in autumn when we have picked all the summer basil
and just made our own fresh pesto. Nothing wrong
with a jar of shop-bought, though, if you haven't got
the time or ingredients to make your own – it will still
do the job.

serves 4

500g button mushrooms, roughly chopped
1 celery stalk, diced
2 potatoes, diced
1 large onion, finely chopped
1 litre of hot vegetable or chicken stock
3-4 tablespoons of olive oil
2 tablespoons of basil pesto
100ml fresh double cream (optional)
salt and pepper

Heat the olive oil in a large saucepan and gently fry the onions and celery for 3 to 4 minutes until soft but not browned.

Add the potatoes and the mushrooms, stir and simmer for 2 more minutes.

Add the hot stock, cover and simmer for half an hour.

Work the soup with a hand blender for 2 minutes until nice and smooth. If you don't have a hand blender, just take the vegetables out of the soup and whiz to a puree in a food processor, then return them to the pan and stir in.

Add the pesto and cream (if using) and continue to simmer very gently for 2 minutes.

Finally taste and adjust the seasoning if necessary with salt and pepper.

*F*akés are a staple part of the Greek diet, especially during winter and Lent. They are ridiculously cheap, incredibly nutritious and extremely tasty. Every Greek housewife will have her own recipe for this hearty, rustic soup and the possibilities for variation are endless. Add any root vegetable diced or grated, add shredded cabbage, chopped courgette… use your imagination.

My dad loved to accompany his bowl of fakés with some crusty bread, a couple of pieces of smoked fish and a glass or three of wine straight from the barrel. This is country food at it's very best.

serves 4

500g brown lentils, rinsed and drained
4 tablespoons of olive oil
1 large red onion, finely chopped
3 cloves of garlic, crushed
1 leek, thinly sliced
1 litre of cold water
1 tablespoon of tomato puree
1 vegetable stock cube
2 tablespoons of dried oregano
salt and pepper

Put olive oil, onions leeks and garlic into a large saucepan and heat gently for 3 minutes so that the vegetables start to soften.

Add the lentils and the water and bring to the boil. When boiling, lower the heat to a moderate simmer, put the lid on the saucepan and leave to cook for about 45 minutes, or until the lentils are soft. The length of time this will take will depend on the freshness of the lentils you're using… the older the lentils, the longer they'll need before they soften. Be aware though, do not continue with the recipe until the lentils are soft enough, because once you have added any salt (there will be some in the stock cube) they will not soften any further… no matter how long you cook them.

Once the lentils have softened, stir in the tomato puree and crumble in the stock cube. Taste and adjust the seasoning with salt and pepper if necessary, then continue simmering for a further 20 minutes. At the end of cooking, add the oregano and stir through.

*W*henever I eat this soup I am instantly transported back to my childhood. It's not the sort of dish you would find in a taverna, but it is home-cooking and Mum would often make it for us in the summer when the tomatoes are ripe and full of flavour. My grandmother's variation was to add some chicken wings to the onions and continue frying until they colour up, then continue with the recipe as it is. The chicken wings are left whole, and float in the soup. They are quite messy to eat, but absolutely delicious.

You can always adapt this and serve the wings on a separate plate if you like.

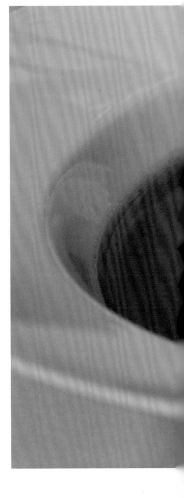

serves 4

2 beef tomatoes, skinned, de-seeded and cut in to 4

1 red onion, finely chopped

1 celery stalk, finely chopped

2 carrots, grated

half a teaspoon of sweet paprika

3 tablespoons of olive oil

1 litre of hot chicken stock

1 tablespoon of dried oregano

a good size bunch of parsley, finely chopped

150g vermicelli or angel's hair pasta

for my grandmother's version

add 12 chicken wings

Heat the olive oil in a saucepan, add the chopped onion and simmer for 2 minutes to soften. (If you are following my grandmother's version, now is the time to sauté the chicken wings).

Add the tomatoes, celery, carrots and paprika. Stir to mix and then pour on the hot chicken stock. Cover and simmer for 30 minutes.

Using a slotted spoon, scoop out half of the vegetables and put them into a mixer or food processor, and whizz until pureed. Stir the pureed vegetables back into the soup.

Add the pasta and herbs and simmer for a few more minutes until the pasta is cooked.

Serve sprinkled with grated parmesan or pecorino and crusty bread.

Vegetable dishes

Piata lahanikon

serves 4

3-4 potatoes boiled with their skins on

3 tablespoons of olive oil

juice of half a lemon

2 spring onions, finely chopped

half a red and half a yellow pepper, chopped

1 tablespoon of good mustard

1 finely chopped sprig of thyme

salt and freshly ground black pepper

While the potatoes are cooking, put the olive oil, lemon juice, mustard, salt and pepper in a small glass jar and shake well to make a dressing.

Skin the potatoes, when cool enough to handle, and break them into a large serving bowl with your fingers. Add the onions, thyme and peppers. Pour the dressing over the potatoes and mix in gently with a wooden spoon.

ripe tomatoes cut into chunks

chunky slices of red onion

green, red and yellow peppers, cut across to create rings

cucumber sliced

Kalamata olives

feta cheese

salt and pepper to taste

olive oil

dried oregano

Simply add all the ingredients except the feta cheese and oregano into a bowl and mix them around with your hands.

Place a nice sized slab of feta cheese on top and sprinkle the oregano over the cheese and salad.

Proportions will, of course, depend on how many people you are serving.

serves 4

1kg slim french beans, cleaned and trimmed
4 tablespoons of olive oil
2 tablespoons of lemon juice
1 garlic clove, crushed
1 large tomato, quartered
salt and pepper

Bring a pan of salted water to the boil and add the beans once boiling briskly. Cook for 8 to 10 minutes until tender but still al-dente

Strain and run some cold water over them to refresh them, then leave to drain well – the drier the better.

Put the rest of the ingredients in a blender and whizz until smooth. Taste and adjust the seasoning with salt and pepper.

Place the beans in a bowl and pour over the sauce. Mix well.

TIP: *We serve this lovely dish in the summer instead of a salad to accompany any grilled meats or fish*

serves 4

500g haloumi, cut into thin slices
1kg baby new potatoes, washed
2 sprigs of fresh thyme
2 cloves of garlic, sliced
150g black Kalamata olives (optional)
250g cherry tomatoes
1 glass of dry white wine
olive oil
fresh rocket leaves
salt and pepper

Heat the oven to 200C

Place the potatoes on a baking tray and sprinkle with olive oil, salt and pepper.

Toss them and bake for half an hour until tender.

Add the rest of the ingredients and bake until the skins of the tomatoes turn colour and begin to split.

Serve warm

serves 4

360g arborio or carnaroli rice

1 red onion, finely chopped

2 cloves garlic, finely chopped

3-4 white mushrooms, finely chopped

half a red pepper, finely chopped

a quarter of a leek, finely chopped

1 cup of fresh parsley, finely chopped

1 glass of white wine

1 bay leaf

3 tablespoons olive oil

750ml of chicken or vegetable stock

Salt and freshly ground black pepper

Pour the olive oil in a non-stick pan and, when hot, add the onions and fry for 2 minutes to soften but not brown. Add the garlic and fry for 1 more minute before adding the mushrooms, peppers, leek and bay leaf and cook for a further 5 minutes.

Add the rice and cook, stir continuously until it becomes shiny. Add the wine (it will splutter and splash to begin with so stand back) and cook until the liquid has dissolved.

Add the stock, a little at a time, to the pan. Season with salt and pepper to taste. Add a little more water if necessary, until the rice is cooked. Stir in the parsley, take the pan off the heat and leave the risotto to rest, covered, for 5 minutes before serving

serves 2

4 beetroots
1 small cinnamon stick
half tablespoon of rock salt
1 bunch rocket, chopped
80-100g feta cheese, crumbled
1 tablespoon hazelnuts, crumbled

for the vinaigrette
2 tablespoons olive oil
1 teaspoon white wine vinegar
1 tablespoon lemon juice
1 spring onion, finely chopped
1 tablespoon fresh mint, chopped
salt and freshly ground black pepper

Pre-heat the oven to 180C.

Place beetroot, cinnamon and salt in foil, make a parcel and then bake for 50 minutes or until the beetroot is cooked.

Meanwhile, put all the vinaigrette ingredients into a mixer and whizz for a couple of minutes. When the beetroot is cool enough to handle, peel and cut into chunks and put them in a bowl and add half of the vinaigrette mixture.

In another bowl, mix remaining vinaigrette with the feta cheese, hazelnuts and rocket.

Each individual serving should be half beetroot mixture topped with half of the feta mixture.

*T*his old, traditional Greek dish is probably my favourite way to eat eggs and one that I have enjoyed since childhood.

Make sure you use the very best eggs you can find and don't skimp on the olive oil.

We are lucky here in the village as we keep our own chickens, so fresh, free-range eggs are always available.

You can use tinned tomatoes when fresh are out of season without losing too much flavour, but if you make this using beautiful fresh, ripe ones you'll have summer on a plate.

serves 8

8 large free-range eggs
1 finely chopped large ripe beef tomato
1 finely chopped red onion
5 tablespoons of olive oil
salt and black pepper
a little oregano
a little feta cheese, crumbled (optional)

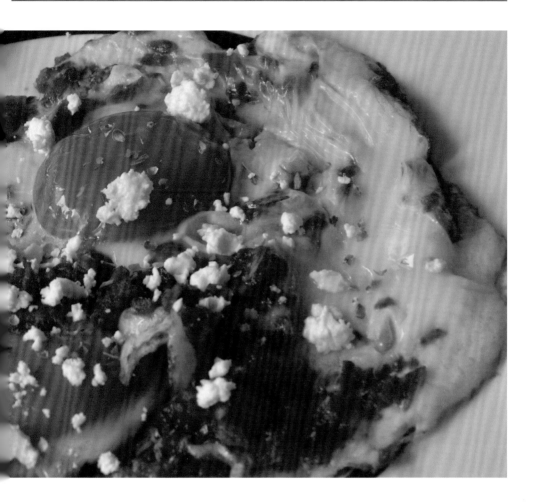

Fry the onion in the olive oil for 3 to 4 minutes then add the chopped tomato and season with salt and pepper.

Simmer gently for 15 to 20 minutes or until the juices of the tomato are absorbed. Crack the eggs into the pan and cook slowly for 5 more minutes.

Turn the heat off and sprinkle the eggs with a little oregano. At this stage, some crumbled feta cheese stirred in will give a lovely flavour.

Dish up your eggs onto a plate and spoon some of the tomato sauce over the top of them.

Serve with crusty bread to mop up those delicious juices for a tasty, nutritious supper or light lunch

I love this simple, delicious recipe. My grandmother used to cook it in the days when no-one could afford meat or fish, but it is so tasty we still eat it today.

TIP: *During cooking you may need to add a little more water if the potatoes haven't softened, but do this a little at a time as you don't want any water left once they're done or you'll have to drain away all those wonderful flavours*

serves 4

1 kilo of potatoes peeled and cut into quarters

I large red onion, finely chopped

5 tablespoons of olive oil

juice of 1 lemon

2 teaspoons of sweet paprika

half teaspoon of chilli flakes

Half a pint of boiling hot chicken or vegetable stock

Pour the olive oil into a large saucepan and fry the onions until golden.

Add the potatoes and fry for a further 2-3 minutes then add the chilli flakes and paprika. Give this a stir and pour in the lemon juice and the stock.

Cover and simmer until the potatoes are tender and the liquid has evaporated, leaving the potatoes in a wonderful rich flavoured oil.

serves 4

250g chickpeas, soaked in cold water overnight

1 green pepper, sliced

2 sweet red peppers, sliced

1 yellow pepper, sliced

1 red onion, finely chopped

3 cloves of garlic, crushed

1 x 250g tin of chopped tomatoes

1 sprig of fresh rosemary, chopped

4 to 5 tablespoons of olive oil

2 bay leaves

half a teaspoon of chilli flakes or cayenne pepper

salt and freshly ground black pepper.

Drain and wash the chickpeas and boil in unsalted water. A froth will form when they start to boil, so remove this with a slotted spoon.

Add the bay leaves, and continue to boil until the chickpeas are tender. Strain them, keeping the cooking liquid (because you might need it later) but discarding the bay leaves.

Meanwhile, in a pan add the olive oil and gently fry the onions and garlic for 3-4 minutes until soft. Add the peppers and cook for another 5 minutes. Add the tomatoes, chilli or cayenne pepper, the rosemary, salt and the freshly ground black pepper.

Simmer for 20 minutes over a low heat

to make a sauce. Place the chickpeas in a baking dish, add the tomato sauce and mix well. If the chickpeas are not covered in the tomato sauce, add some of their cooking liquid to cover them.

Preheat your oven to 180C and bake for 40 minutes.

TIP: *If the dish looks dry during baking, add some more of the chickpea cooking liquid*

serves 4

500g of fresh courgettes, sliced

200g of feta cheese

2 beef tomatoes, sliced

1 cup of olive oil

1 teaspoon of chilli flakes

salt and freshly ground black pepper

a handful of chopped fresh herbs, such as parsley, basil and thyme

Lightly oil a baking tray and cover with the tomato slices. Season with the salt, pepper and half of the fresh herb mixture.

Place the courgette slices on top, crumble the feta cheese over them and sprinkle on the rest of herbs and the chilli flakes. Pour on the olive oil and bake in a medium hot oven for 30 minutes, or until the courgettes are tender.

serves 4

300g brown lentils
1 beef tomato, diced
2 bay leaves
2 red onions, finely chopped
1 tablespoon dried oregano
half teaspoon chilli flakes
salt and black pepper

for the dressing
juice from half of a lemon
1 tablespoon of Dijon mustard
2 spring onions, finely chopped
1 bunch of dill, finely chopped
3-4 tablespoons of olive oil

Put the lentils, oregano, tomatoes, onions and chilli flakes into a large saucepan. Cover with cold unsalted water and boil for 45 minutes until the lentils are soft.

Discard the bay leaves, add salt and pepper and simmer for 3 more minutes. Take the pan off the heat.

In a separate bowl mix the dressing ingredients together.

Add them to your lentils, mix with a wooden spoon, put the lid back on and leave the dish to rest for 5 minutes.

Serve with fresh crusty bread.

This is a favourite during Lent, when the Orthodox religion here in Greece forbids meat, fish or dairy produce for the 40 days before Easter. Some traditionalists still observe the full 40 days of fasting, but over the years Greeks have become more and more relaxed about it. Having said that, there won't be a household that doesn't observe Nistia (fasting) during Megali Evdomada (the week before Easter). Even restaurants and tavernas will have a wide selection of Nistissima (Lentern dishes) for their customers and this dish will be among them.

Beautiful fresh globe artichokes are in abundance here during Lent, and the dill is plentiful as it grows wild in the ditches and hedgerows and you can collect it by the armful. You can still make this dish with frozen or canned artichokes ...but it won't taste nearly as good.

serves 4

8 artichoke hearts
3 tablespoons of olive oil
2 medium red onions, finely chopped
4 spring onions, finely chopped
juice of 2 lemons
8 baby onions, peeled and left whole
2 carrots, sliced
3 tablespoons plain flour
3 tablespoons of fresh dill, finely chopped
8 small new potatoes
salt and freshly ground black pepper

Heat the olive oil in a saucepan, add all the onions and fry for 3 minutes.

Add the carrots and fry for 1 more minute.

Sprinkle with the flour and fry for another minute, then add 2 normal sized coffee mugs of water and bring to the boil.

Add the artichokes with the stem facing up, the dill, lemon juice, salt and pepper.

Simmer for 5 minutes before adding the new potatoes.

Simmer until the vegetables are tender and the sauce has thickened.

Two medium potatoes per person, peeled and sliced roughly into quarters

Approximately 1 tablespoon of olive oil for every three potatoes

Equivalent amount of lemon juice

Dried oregano

Freshly ground salt and black pepper

Heat an oven to 180C

Place the sliced potatoes in a baking dish and drizzle with the oil and lemon juice so they are all covered.

Sprinkle with oregano and add the salt and pepper.

Cook for approximately an hour until they are soft, turning them after 30 minutes.

If they dry out add a little water to keep them moist

serves 6 as a dip

1 medium sized cucumber

250g Greek yoghurt

2 garlic cloves, peeled and crushed with sprout removed (you can use just one if you wish –depending on preference)

2 tablespoons of olive oil

2 tablespoons of white wine vinegar

salt to taste

Peel cucumber, but leave some green strips for colour and remove seeds and grate coarsely.

Sprinkle with salt and compress it using a heavy weight in a strainer for about 20 minutes, then squeeze out remaining liquid with your hands.

Mix cucumber, garlic, vinegar and salt, then fold in the yoghurt and olive oil.

*A*bsolutely the most traditional accompaniment for fish or seafood here in Greece. Skordalia is also an important part of many festive meals throughout the year here. There isn't a household in Greece that doesn't prepare fish and skordalia on March 25th to celebrate National Independence Day. Salt-cod and skordalia is also the traditional meal the entire country enjoys on Palm Sunday. As we would always be serving fish with the skordalia, we flavour the water that the potatoes are boiled in by adding the fish head and trimmings, rather than salt. If you don't have a fish head or trimmings to hand, don't worry...a fish stock cube will do the same job for you.

serves 4 to 6 as an accompaniment

1 kilo of potatoes, unpeeled, scrubbed and left whole

Enough fish stock to cover the potatoes

A whole head of garlic (you can reduce this to taste, but not by much if you want to go authentic)

Juice of 2 unwaxed lemons

A water glass of olive oil (you may not need it all)

Put the potatoes into cold water with the stock cube (or fish head and trimmings if you're going traditional) and bring to the boil. While the potatoes are boiling, peel the garlic and pound the cloves to a smooth paste with a mortar and pestle. Boil the potatoes until soft, then drain and leave to get cool enough to handle. Once cooled a little, peel the skins and put the potatoes into a large pan with the garlic paste. Start to mash the potatoes and garlic together and, when well mixed, gently start pouring in a little olive oil and some of the lemon juice. Mix again, then continue adding more oil

and juice, always a little at a time, checking for taste and consistency as you go. You are looking for a strong garlic flavour, tempered with the sharpness of the lemon, and a very smooth, soft consistency...thinner than mash potato, but not sloppy. The garlic flavour will intensify as the skordalia rests, so be warned. When you have the flavour and consistency you want, spoon the Skordalia in to a serving dish, drizzle with olive oil and leave to cool before serving.

TIP: *Skordalia can be quite heavy on the digestion, so to solve this I recommend removing the little sprout that you'll find in the centre of the cloves before you pound them. It works.*

Whether eaten as street food, starter, party-fare or a main course, Spanakotyropita is one of the nation's most loved favourites. It's also a firm winner in the restaurant, even if it is another one of the unpronounceable dishes.

Creamy feta cheese is a natural partner to lovely fresh spinach and the addition of parsley, dill and mint bring out the best in both flavours. A dairy-free version of this pie is also very popular, especially during Lent...we simply leave out the feta cheese, but bulk up on the other ingredients. Absolutely delicious, whichever way you decide to cook it.

800g of chopped, fresh spinach
1 large red onion finely chopped
4 spring onions finely chopped
1 cup of chopped fresh dill
1 cup chopped fresh parsley
1 handful chopped fresh mint
2 eggs, beaten
200g crumbled feta cheese
3 tablespoons of olive oil
salt and freshly ground black pepper
1 packet filo pastry

Heat oven to 180C

Place olive oil in a large sauce pan, add all the onions and fry gently for 5 minutes until softened. Add spinach and cook until all juices have evaporated.

Take the pan off the heat and let the mixture cool for 5 minutes. Add feta cheese, chopped herbs and beaten eggs and mix well with a wooden spoon. Season to taste, with salt and pepper.

Layer half of your filo pastry sheets in the bottom of a lightly oiled baking dish, brushing every one of them with olive oil as you go. Spread the spinach mixture on top, and layer the rest of the filo pastry over the top, again brushing each sheet with olive oil.

Brush the top sheet with some more olive oil and sprinkle with a handful of water. With a sharp knife slit the top pastry sheets into squares. Bake for 50 minutes, or until the filo becomes nice and golden.

▶ A fabulous way of making the humble pea a talking point at the table is to heat a good glug of olive oil in a wide, shallow pan (a frying pan is fine) and gently soften some thinly sliced onion (chopped doesn't work so well).

When the onion's soft, but not coloured, put the required quantity of peas in to the pan and add chopped mint and dill. Stir to mix well, then pour on enough hot vegetable stock to half cover the ingredients. Simmer very slowly, stirring occasionally, until the peas are tender and the liquid has evaporated, leaving a lovely flavoured oil coating the peas.

The result is stunning.

▶ A similarly impressive way of enhancing carrots is to peel and cut them into thin batons, and slice some fresh ginger into julienne strips. Heat a good glug of olive oil, but in a saucepan this time, and gently sweat the juliennes of fresh ginger until the aroma is released. Then add the carrot batons, a little lemon zest and some lemon juice, and stir to mix well. Add very little hot vegetable or chicken stock, cover, and cook until the carrots are tender and the liquid evaporated, checking the liquid levels as you go. If you run out of liquid before the carrots are cooked, just continue adding stock, but a little at a time.

You will never plain boil carrots again once you've tried this. Other flavours can be used in the same way . . . experiment and use your imagination according to the meat or fish that you want to accompany. For instance, you can replace the ginger with garlic, and the lemon zest with cumin for a completely different taste... I use this combination a lot in the restaurant.

Seafood

Thalassina

Mobile fishmonger in Zakynthos town, 1986

*C*an anything conjure up the simplicity and wonderful flavours of Greece better than a plate of perfectly fried calamari? The ultimate summer treat…a plate of sizzling calamari and a glass of ice-cold retsina after a mid-day swim.

serves 4

1kg calamari fresh or frozen, cut into thick rings
3-4 tablespoons of plain flour
enough vegetable oil to deep fry
salt and pepper

Put flour, salt and pepper into a clean plastic bag, add the calamari and shake well so all the rings are floured.

In a deep frying pan or a deep-fat fryer, heat the oil until it starts smoking. Take a few rings at a time, shake them well to get rid of any excess flour and fry for 2 minutes. Drain on kitchen paper to absorb any excess oil, keep them warm and fry the next batch.

Nothing beats a plate of crisply fried, tender calamari so, for a perfect outcome take care not to overcrowd the pan (the calamari will not crisp up) and do not cook for any longer than 2 minutes or the calamari will go tough.

TIP: *Try these accompanied with Skordalia (see page 38) and a village salad (see page 23) and you have a meal fit for a king.*

*T*his recipe has evolved over some time at the taverna and
has been a standard favourite now for many years.
The sauce here is absolutely delicious, and needs plenty of fresh
crusty bread to mop it up …alternatively a spoon.

serves 4

**1kg fresh mussels. discard broken ones
or any that stay open after a gentle tap,
remove beards from side of shell and scrape
off any barnacles**

2 spring onions, finely chopped

3 garlic cloves, finely chopped

1 teaspoon of smoked paprika

half a pint dry white wine

1 celery stalk, finely chopped

**a good handful of fresh parsley, finely
chopped**

1 vegetable stock cube

3 tablespoons of olive oil

Heat the oil in a large cooking pan and gently
fry the spring onions for 2 minutes.

Add the garlic and fry for 2 more minutes.

Then add the celery, parsley, paprika, wine
and stock cube.

Bring to the boil, reduce heat, and simmer
uncovered for 20 minutes.

Add the mussels, put the lid on and cook
until they have opened up. Discard any that
did not open.

Without doubt this is the most popular fish dish in Corfu and no taverna menu there is complete without it. Skate is the first choice fish for bourdeto because of the rich texture it imparts to the finished sauce, but cod makes a good substitute and is sometimes more easily available, so go with whichever looks best at the fishmongers. A good bourdeto should be quite spicy, but if you prefer something a little milder, adjust the amount of cayenne you use. You won't have a traditional bourdeto, but you'll still have a delicious version of it.

serves 4

1kg of skate or cod, cut into portions
1 medium to small red onion, finely sliced
3 cloves of garlic, finely chopped
half teaspoon of cayenne pepper
1 teaspoon of paprika
juice of 1 lemon
200ml of hot water
a handful of chopped fresh parsley
salt and black pepper
4-5 tablespoons of olive oil.

Heat the olive oil in a wide, shallow cooking pan and when it's hot add the onions. Fry for 2 minutes.

Add the chopped garlic and fry for 1 more minute. Then add the cayenne pepper and paprika, stirring for a few seconds until their aroma is released.

Add the lemon juice and water and simmer for 10 minutes.

Place the fish in the pan and spoon the juices all over the fish. Sprinkle with parsley and cover with the lid.

Simmer for 15 to 20 minutes until the fish is tender and cooked.

serves 4

**4 cod fillets about 200g each
(or any other white fleshy fish)**

1 large red onion, thinly sliced

2 bay leaves

1 cup of chopped fresh parsley

**1 wine glass filled half with dry Martini and
half with dry white wine**

150ml of vegetable or fish stock

4 to 5 tablespoons of double cream

a knob of butter

2 tablespoons of olive oil

black and white pepper

*A friend of mine cooked this recipe
for me many years ago, and I was
so impressed with the simplicity and
the flavours that I developed it for the
taverna and have been cooking it ever
since.*

Heat the olive oil and butter in a large
cooking pan and gently fry the onion for 3 to
4 minutes until soft but not brown.

Add the wine and Martini mixture and
simmer for a couple of minutes until the
alcohol evaporates. Add the bay leaves
and fish, sprinkle with the black and white
pepper, pour on enough stock to cover and
simmer for 10 minutes.

Add the cream and chopped parsley. Shake
the pan and simmer for 1 more minute.

*T*his is a typical dish from Corfu and was my grandad's favourite fish dish.

Traditionally we would use dried salted cod, but it works equally as well with fresh cod too... just a different intensity of flavour.

Grandad would get some fresh crusty bread, break it into small pieces and put it in the sauce. He'd leave the bread soaking for a minute or two while he would enjoy sipping at his glass of retsina and then, when the bread had absorbed so much of the juices that it was completely soft, he would use his soup spoon to get out a little bread, a small piece of potato and cod, those beautiful juices... and he was in heaven.

serves 4

4 pieces filleted fresh cod, or dried salted cod

3 potatoes cut in round slices 1cm thick

3 to 4 tablespoons of olive oil

salt and white pepper

1 bay leaf

plenty of chopped fresh parsley

4 garlic cloves, sliced thinly

juice of half a lemon

If using dried salt cod you will need to prepare it 24 hours in advance.

Place the fillets in cold water and leave at room temperature, changing the water at least 3 times. This will reconstitute and de-salt the cod. Drain very well, dry with kitchen paper and then remove the skin. Do not use salt, but season just with white pepper and keep aside.

If using fresh cod, make sure the fish is dry

(pat with kitchen paper). Season with salt and white pepper and keep aside.

In a heavy cooking pan add the olive oil and garlic and simmer over a low heat for 2 minutes. Do not let it brown.

Add the potato slices and sauté for 3 more minutes. Then add the bay leaf, just enough water to cover the potatoes and simmer for 10 minutes.

Lay the cod fillets on top of the other ingredients and cook for another 6 to 8 minutes with the lid on.

Add the chopped parsley and pour in the lemon juice, cover and take off the heat. Shake the pan a little so that the lemon juice and parsley get well mixed in (don't stir or you will break up the fish) and leave for 5 minutes for the fish to absorb the aroma and flavours of the lemon and parsley, and serve.

The combination of prawn and bacon is a classic, but the marinade adds a subtle background heat which intensifies with the grilling. Do this on charcoal if you possibly can and, as a suggestion, serve with a mixed green salad and vegetable risotto (see page 26).

serves 4

16 king prawns, whole
juice of half a lemon
a few chilli flakes or a little cayenne pepper
salt
1-2 tablespoons of olive oil
8 rashers of bacon

TIP: You will find it easier to skewer the prawns through the tail first and then the head

Make your marinade by mixing the lemon juice, cayenne pepper or chilli, olive oil and salt in a bowl.

Peel the prawns leaving the heads and tails on. With a cocktail stick or toothpick, carefully remove the black vein from the top of the prawns.

Place them in a shallow dish and pour over the marinade, cover with cling film and put in the fridge for at least 1 hour.

Pre-heat the grill or light the barbecue.

Remove the prawns from the marinade and put it to one side for basting later and put the prawns onto skewers (if you are using bamboo skewers soak them in water for 30 minutes before using, also soak some cocktail sticks or toothpicks) allow 4 prawns per skewer.

Wrap 2 rashers of bacon around the whole skewer, enclosing the prawns, and secure with cocktail sticks or toothpicks. Place the skewers under the grill or on the barbecue and grill for 5 minutes each side, basting with the rest of the marinade.

serves 4

16 king prawns, peeled (remove black intestinal vein across the back)

2 garlic cloves, crushed

half a teaspoon of chilli flakes

100g crumbled feta cheese

a bunch of chopped fresh parsley

1 ripe beef tomato, diced

salt and pepper

olive oil

A saganaki is any dish cooked in the traditional saganaki pan. This is a small shallow frying pan with a handle either side, usually made from cast iron. A frying pan works equally as well though, in fact, most Greek housewives will make their saganakis in a frying pan these days.

Heat the olive oil in a frying pan and then add garlic and chilli flakes and simmer for 2 to 3 minutes.

Scoop them out of the pan using a slotted spoon and discard.

Add your diced tomato, salt, pepper and a little water and simmer for 15 minutes to make a sauce. Add the peeled prawns and cook for a further 6 minutes, turning the

prawns once. They will turn a lovely pink colour.

If the sauce starts to dry out, add a little hot water, but only if necessary. The sauce should be thick, but not runny.

Add the chopped parsley and crumbled feta cheese and cook for another minute.

Serve with crusty bread.

*K*olios is a smooth, oily Mediterranean fish, and a member of the Mackerel family. They are so similar that, whilst you won't find Kolios, Mackerel can be substituted perfectly and will be just as tasty. Kolios is a very economical fish, at it's best and most abundant during the height of the summer, which is when we eat it alot! There is a very wise old Greek saying. Phonetically for you it would read: Kathe pramma sto kairo, kai o Kolios sto Avgousto!.... which translates to "Everything in it's season...and Kolios in August!" A crisp green salad (and a glass of cold wine!) is all you need to accompany this simple but delicious dish.

serves 4

4 whole large mackerel, filleted
1 ripe beef tomato, sliced into 4
plenty of fresh dill and parsley, finely
chopped
1 tablespoon of dried oregano
salt and black pepper
4-5 tablespoons of olive oil

Heat the oven to 200C

Lay a sheet of greaseproof paper on a baking tray and sprinkle with half of the dill and parsley mixture.

Place the fillets on top of the herbs and add the tomato slices, 1 on each fillet. Add the

TIP: *As a variation you can try adding some thinly sliced potatoes. Place them on the greaseproof paper first, then follow the recipe as shown, squeezing the juice of half a lemon over the dish before cooking. The potatoes are particularly tasty like this as they absorb all the flavours*

rest of the herbs, salt and pepper, and bake for 30 minutes.

● For greater authenticity we would bake the fish whole and eat it off the bone, but for finer dining you can fillet the fish

Chicken

Kotopoulo

In 1983 Diana and I were working in Garitsa, a suburb of Corfu Town, my father's birthplace. The birth of our first niece or nephew was imminent and every afternoon on our break Diana would run to the little bookshop on the corner to phone England to find out if there was any news.

Remember, in those days there were no mobile phones. In fact, the only phone in the area was in that bookshop.

One afternoon she came back with the news we'd been waiting for... we were uncle and aunty to a niece.

In celebration I cooked this dish. I adapted the classic Greek lemonato recipe and added potatoes to it...and this variation has remained known as Chicken Zoe-Louise in our family ever since. It is one of the best-selling specials that I have at The Olive Tree and rightly so. The potatoes absorb all the wonderful lemony, herby flavours of the chicken and are so delicious that you'll never have enough.

Zoe-Louise with Hee Haw

serves 4

1 whole fresh chicken, cut into 4 portions

1 tablespoon flour for dusting

3-4 large potatoes, cut into 4 lengthwise

2 leeks, chopped

2 cloves garlic, crushed

3-4 tablespoon olive oil

salt and fresh black pepper

juice from 1 lemon, plus a little of the zest

1 tablespoon of dried oregano

3 to 4 sprigs of fresh thyme

1 cup fresh parsley, chopped

Season chicken with salt and pepper and dust with some flour on both sides.

Heat the olive oil in a frying pan and colour the chicken pieces on both sides. Depending

on the size of your frying pan you may have to do this in batches.

When nicely golden, take them out of the frying pan and place in a large shallow saucepan or sauté pan.

Fry the potato pieces in the same oil until they start to get a nice colour. Remove and put with the chicken pieces.

Add the chopped leeks and the crushed garlic to the frying pan and fry for 3 to 4 minutes until the leeks are soft and turning colour.

Add this to the chicken and potatoes in the saucepan, add a little water and adjust the seasoning and simmer for half an hour.

Add the lemon juice and zest and simmer for another 10 minutes.

Finally add the oregano, thyme and parsley, shake the pan to mix and remove it from the heat. Let it rest for 10 minutes before serving to allow the flavours of the herbs to infuse the sauce.

Zoe-Louise with some souvlaki horns

*I*am constantly trying to create
different dishes that will work well
in the taverna and this one ticks all the
boxes.

It is full of all the tastes and colours
of Greek summer, is amazingly
simple and quick to make (which is
great for the cook) and bursts with
Mediterranean flavours (even better
for the diner) and appears regularly
with success on our specials board.

serves 4

4 fresh chicken fillets

1 finely chopped onion

1 green, 1 red and 1 yellow pepper, cut into strips

2 cloves of garlic, crushed

1 tablespoon pesto

1 glass of dry white wine

half teaspoon chilli flakes

olive oil

salt and pepper

Heat the olive oil in a frying pan, add the chicken fillets and brown on both sides. Remove with a slotted spoon and place them into a pan that has a lid.

Add the onions to the frying pan and sauté gently for 2 minutes before adding the garlic and the coloured peppers and cooking for a further 5 minutes.

Add the wine, a little water and sprinkle in the chilli flakes. Stir well, bring to the boil and then pour over the chicken fillets in the pan.

Cover and then simmer for half an hour.

Add the pesto and cook for 2-3 more minutes until the pesto is dissolved into the sauce. Adjust seasoning with salt and pepper as necessary.

*T*his is one of my mum's dishes that I've tweaked a little for the modern-day palate.

When mum cooked it she would use whole chicken pieces, left on the bone. You can too but be prepared to get messy eating off the bone...you won't be able to avoid it if you eat this Greek-style.

serves 4

4 chicken fillets, cut into chunks

4 garlic cloves, finely chopped

2 rashers of bacon, chopped

a large handful of fresh rosemary, thyme and parsley, all finely chopped

2 tablespoons of olive oil

2 tablespoons of butter

half a teaspoon of smoked paprika

250ml hot vegetable stock

2 tablespoons of grated kefalotiri cheese (parmesan makes a good substitute)

salt and pepper.

We have a slightly saucy saying that is, nevertheless, true:

"Fish, chicken and women are best enjoyed using your hands"

Heat the olive oil and butter in a large cooking pot and, when hot, add the chicken pieces and sauté until they are browned all over.

Add garlic and bacon and fry for 2 more minutes.

Reduce the heat, add the chopped herbs, smoked paprika, season with salt and pepper and simmer for 3 to 4 minutes.

Add the hot stock and simmer slowly for 30 minutes.

Remove from the heat, sprinkle all over with parmesan cheese and leave to rest for 5 minutes before serving.

Yaourtlou is a vintage recipe I remember being very popular when I was a small boy and is currently, justifiably in my opinion, enjoying a revival.

The actual word means 'yoghurtey', and is virtually unpronounceable for most Western Europeans. Diana always knows when someone wants to order this from the menu...they'll start by saying "I'll never be able to say this, but..." So, as a help, phonetically, it is ya-OO-URT-lew... have a go.

It has been an extremely successful addition to our menu and has proved a firm favourite, despite the name. In the taverna I use chicken for the dish, but it works equally as well with pork and also bifteki.

(See page 84 for bifteki recipe)

serves 4

4 chicken fillets cut into thick 3-4cm strips
1 teaspoon of sweet paprika
half teaspoon of chilli flakes
1 teaspoon of salt
3 tablespoons of olive oil
2 tablespoons of Greek honey
3 tablespoons of Greek yoghurt

Place chicken and the rest of the ingredients except the yoghurt into a shallow dish, rub them with your fingers so they are all coated evenly, cover with cling film and leave them in the fridge for at least an hour.

If time allows leave them overnight. The longer they stay in the marinade the better.

Heat a little olive oil in a frying pan and fry the chicken gently for 7 to 8 minutes, then turn them over another seven minutes or until chicken is cooked through.

You can test if they are cooked through by slicing the thickest part of the strip.

When cooked remove the pan from the heat

TIP: *Make sure you only use the Greek full fat yoghurt for this dish or you will have a runny, unattractive sauce.*

add your yoghurt and stir until the yoghurt melts and becomes creamy.

You can serve with mushroom or vegetable risotto or a village salad

The first time I tasted this dish was in a small bistro in Pangrati, an area in the centre of Athens where my cousins live. Of course, if you can't find the Greek brandy Metaxa, you can use any other kind of brandy… just keep it economical. You don't need to splash out on a cognac to get the best results.

Pasta is the perfect accompaniment to this dish and shapes are even better as they will catch all the beautiful sauce.

serves 4

4 chicken fillets, cut into thick strips

40g butter

3 to 4 tablespoons of olive oil

3 spring onions, finely chopped

150ml dry white wine

3 tablespoons of Metaxa or 3-star brandy

2 egg yolks, beaten

300ml double cream

a handful of finely chopped flat leaf parsley
salt and plenty of black pepper

Melt the butter into the olive oil in a heavy bottomed casserole pan and, when hot, put in the chicken fillet strips and sauté for a few minutes until evenly browned. Add the chopped spring onion and fry for a further 2 minutes.

Pour the wine into the brandy and mix together before adding to the pan. Ignite immediately and when the flames have died down cover, reduce the heat and simmer for 15 minutes until the chicken is cooked through. Remove from the heat.

Beat the egg yolks and cream together, and blend into the casserole pan, stirring well.

Stir in the chopped parsley and season with salt and plenty of black pepper to taste.

*T*he souvlaki (which means skewer) is the national street food of Greece and, depending on size and content, can be anything from a small takeaway snack to a sit-down main meal. It happens to be my personal favourite late-night nibble after a busy evening at the taverna.

The variations for souvlaki are endless…use your imagination, and the vegetables of your choice.

4 portions

4 chicken breasts or pork loins cut into 6 cubes each

8 skewers (bamboo or otherwise)

2 onions, sliced into chunks

2 green peppers cut into large squares

4 rashers of streaky bacon

for the marinade

3 tablespoons of olive oil

1 tablespoon of mustard

1 teaspoon of sweet paprika

2 teaspoons of dried oregano

juice of 1 lemon

salt and pepper

Assemble your souvlakia by threading in turn one piece of onion, then one piece of green pepper and then one piece of chicken onto the skewer…then repeat until the skewer is almost full. Finally wind a rasher of bacon around the assembled skewer.

Barbecue over hot coals for 15 to 20 minutes until the chicken is cooked, basting with any remaining marinade.

You can also cook this under the grill in the same way.

Mix all the marinade ingredients together, put in a stainless steel or glass bowl and add the chicken cubes.

Toss the chicken in the marinade to coat well, cover with cling film and leave for at least one hour at room temperature.

When ready to use, remove the chicken pieces but keep the marinade.

If using bamboo skewers, soak them for 10 minutes in a bowl of cold water before use.

Left, the finished article and right, Asadullah shows how it's done

TIP: *With the increasing awareness of healthy food choices, I have replaced the traditional use of pork in this recipe with marinated chicken breast as a non-fat alternative.*

As a consequence, the souvlakia will need constant basting during the cooking time to keep the meat moist and succulent. If you decide to go traditional and use pork, you'll follow the recipe in exactly the same way, but leave out the bacon because pork has enough fat of its own

*I*n our village of Kypseli they grow the most succulent plum tomatoes which are conveniently in season at the hottest time of the summer. I say conveniently, because it means we have the ideal conditions for the sun-drying process as well as the perfect produce for it.

We always buy plenty and Diana prepares rows and rows of them under fine netting, which keeps the insects off but still allows the sunshine do its job.

She bottles them in our own organic olive oil with a few leaves of basil from our garden for even more aroma.

After all her hard work, the least I could do was create a recipe that would burst with all that bottled sunshine and this one does that just perfectly.

serves 4

1 whole chicken cut in to 4 portions

1 large red onion, chopped

4 garlic cloves, crushed

60g sun-dried tomatoes, drained and chopped

two large ripe tomatoes, skinned and diced or 400g can of chopped tomatoes

1 teaspoon of dried oregano

1 red pepper, deseeded and finely chopped

handful of chopped parsley

1 teaspoon of chilli flakes

4 tablespoons of olive oil

salt and pepper

Dust the chicken pieces in lightly seasoned flour.

Heat the olive oil in a flameproof casserole dish or large sauté pan and, when hot, brown the chicken pieces on both sides. Remove the chicken and keep warm.

In the same pan add the onions, garlic and chopped pepper and fry for a few minutes until brown.

Add the chilli flakes, oregano, sun-dried tomatoes and the fresh tomatoes or the can of tomatoes with its juices, scraping and stirring in any crispy bits off the bottom of the pan as you go. Season with salt and

pepper and bring to the boil.

Put the chicken pieces back into the pan, reduce the heat, cover and simmer for 1 hour stirring occasionally, until the chicken is tender.

Add the fresh parsley and simmer for 2 more minutes.

TIP: *Don't be tempted to add more liquid when returning the chicken to the pan with the reduction – once covered, cooking will produce more than enough juice if using canned tomatoes. If using fresh tomatoes keep an eye on liquid levels, adding small amounts of hot water to keep the dish moist.*

A ny pie is always tastiest when it has cooled, so leave for a while before serving... all you'll need with this one is a crisp green salad to accompany and a glass of chilled white wine.

serves 6

1 packet filo pastry

30g butter

180g boneless chicken, cut into very small cubes

140g button mushrooms, sliced

salt and pepper

30g plain flour

3 cups milk

80g kefalotiri or pecorino cheese, grated (any strong flavoured, hard cheese will be a fine substitute)

a little fresh ground nutmeg

olive oil

Heat oven to 180C

Heat the butter in a pan and when it starts smoking add the chicken and mushrooms.

Fry them on a high heat for 3 to 4 minutes, season with salt and pepper and then add the flour.

Cook for 1 more minute, stirring continuously to avoid lumps. Reduce the heat, add the milk and continue to stir until the sauce thickens.

Take the pan off the heat completely, add the cheese and nutmeg, adjust the seasoning and let it cool a little.

Open your filo pastry and choose a pie dish that is slightly smaller than the pastry so

you'll have extra to fold over to make your pie.

Layer half of the packet on the bottom of a lightly oiled pie dish, brushing each sheet with olive oil as you go.

Gently pour in the pie filling. Layer the top half of the pie as you did the bottom, brushing every sheet of pastry with olive oil.

Brush the edges of the excess pastry with water so that they will stick together, turn them in on each other and press together to form your pie.

Brush the top sheet of filo with olive oil, sprinkle with a little water and, using a sharp

TIP: *Filo pastry dries out fairly quickly, so make sure you keep any you are not working with covered with a clean, slightly damp cloth until you need it to prevent it going flaky.*
Don't be tempted to skimp on the olive oil brushing of the pastry... your pie will be dry and the end result will suffer.

knife, slit the top filo sheets into squared portions. Bake in the middle of the oven for 50 to 60 minutes until golden brown.

*C*ooking chicken like this ensures that you'll always end up with lovely crispy skin… so, not a recipe for those on a diet.

The chicken stays moist inside though, soaking up all the flavours of the lovely garlicky, lemony oil.

I love this recipe for its simplicity and adaptability.

While the method remains the same, by changing the ingredients you can have a different flavoured dish every time.

One of our favourites at home is to swap the paprika for some finely chopped fresh rosemary or thyme…it smells and tastes delicious.

serves 4

1 chicken, skin on, cut into 4 portions or use 4 chicken portions of your choice

2 tablespoons of plain flour

1 teaspoon of sweet paprika

salt and pepper

4 knobs of butter

4 tablespoons of olive oil

juice of 1 lemon

2 garlic cloves, crushed

Heat the oven to 200C

Put half of the butter (2 knobs) and half of the olive oil (2 tablespoons) in a roasting dish and put in the oven to heat.

Mix the flour, paprika, salt and pepper together in a bowl and toss the chicken pieces in this mixture to coat well. Shake off any excess flour and place, skin side down, in the hot oil and butter and bake for 20 minutes.

Meanwhile, put the other half of the olive oil and butter into a small frying pan to heat.

When the butter has melted into the oil add the crushed garlic and lemon juice and cook for about a minute until the garlic has released all of its aroma but has not turned brown.

Turn the chicken pieces and pour the hot, garlic-flavoured butter mixture over them. Bake for 30 minutes, or until the chicken is golden and cooked through.

Minced Meat

Kimas

serves 6

for the meatballs

500g of lean minced beef
250g of lean minced pork
1 red onion, grated
3 cloves of garlic, finely chopped
a handful of fresh parsley and mint, finely chopped
2 teaspoons of ground cumin
1 tablespoon of dried oregano
2 free-range eggs, lightly beaten
3 to 4 tablespoons of breadcrumbs
2 tablespoons of olive oil
salt and black pepper

for the rest of the dish

2 onions, sliced
four tablespoons plus 1 tablespoon of olive oil
2 cloves of garlic, finely chopped
a handful of fresh parsley, finely chopped
1 teaspoon of paprika
2 free range eggs, beaten
600g Greek yoghurt
salt and black pepper

*T*hese little meatballs are bursting with flavour and the soft sauce that they're finished in compliments them beautifully. I discovered this recipe fairly recently over on the mainland while visiting my mum's cousin. She served this to me with her home-made fusilli. It was divine. You can accompany this dish with rice if you prefer and it's even great served simply with a salad.

Put all the ingredients for the meatballs into a large bowl, and knead together with your hands until well mixed. Leave to one side. Then heat oven to 200C.

Heat the four tablespoons of olive oil in a frying pan and, when hot, sauté the sliced onion for 2 to 3 minutes.

Add the chopped parsley and season with salt and pepper.

Remove the frying pan from the heat and pour the contents into a good-sized baking dish.

Take the meat mixture and form into balls, about the size of a golf ball or slightly larger (it should make around 30). Place the meatballs on top of the onion mixture in the baking dish.

Sprinkle a little water over the meatballs and bake in the oven for 30 minutes.

Meanwhile, put the beaten eggs into a clean bowl and add the yoghurt, chopped garlic, paprika, salt and pepper, and the 1 tablespoon of olive oil. Mix lightly with a wooden spoon.

Once the meatballs have been cooking for 30 minutes, take the baking dish out of the oven, gently stir around the meatballs, then pour the yoghurt sauce mixture all over them.

Return to the oven and bake for a further 10 minutes until the yoghurt starts to form a light crust, but is not solidified – resembling a béchamel sauce.

Take out of the oven and leave to rest for 5 minutes before serving.

*P*ossibly the most famous dish in the
Greek cuisine, and so worth all the effort
(and washing up). You will use almost every
pan and utensil in your kitchen during the
preparation, but it's easy after that.

Although the classic recipe is for aubergines
with minced meat, there are as many
variations of moussaka as there are of
shepherd's pie…some people add sliced
potato, others sliced courgette and some add
both.

A traditional moussaka would have the
aubergines fried first and makes this richest
of dishes even heavier. One summer day,
years ago, I came home from the taverna
for lunch and a siesta. The previous day we
had enjoyed a barbecue with friends, and
there were some chargrilled aubergine slices
left over. Diana had decided to experiment
and make use of them in a moussaka. It was
so delicious and light, we have grilled our
aubergines ever since.

serves 6

3 good-sized aubergines, cut into 1cm slices

50g of grated pecorino or other strong
flavoured cheese

for the meat sauce

600-700g of lean minced beef

1 large red onion, finely chopped

3 garlic cloves, crushed

250g tin of chopped tomatoes

1 tablespoon of tomato puree

2 cinnamon sticks

a pinch of ground cloves

1 tablespoon of oregano

salt and pepper

3 to 4 tablespoons of olive oil

1 glass red wine

1 tablespoon of Worcestershire sauce is optional

for the béchamel sauce

100g flour

100g butter

2 large free-range eggs, whisked

700ml of warm milk

salt and pepper

half a teaspoon of grated nutmeg

50g grated pecorino or other strong flavoured cheese

Cooking instructions on pages 80 and 81

Sprinkle the aubergine slices with salt and leave them in a colander for 30 minutes until their bitter juices have drained out. Rinse in cold water and dry them well on kitchen paper.

Brush the aubergine slices with plenty of olive oil (they absorb a lot during cooking), season both sides with a little salt and pepper and grill them until they are nicely browned.

Heat the oven to 200C

In the meantime prepare your meat sauce. Heat the olive oil in a large saucepan, add the onions and garlic and sauté until golden. Add the cinnamon sticks and cook for 1 more minute to release the aroma.

Add the minced meat and cook, stirring frequently, until all the meat juices are absorbed and the mince is nice and crumbly.

Add the wine, tomato puree, chopped tomatoes and season with salt and pepper.

Cook for 30 minutes until the liquid is absorbed. Add ground cloves and stir well.

While the meat sauce is cooking, you can be making your béchamel sauce.

Melt the butter in a thick-bottomed saucepan. Stir in the flour and cook for 3 to 4 minutes, stirring constantly to prevent any lumps forming. The mixture should be thick and smooth.

Remove from the heat and pour the warm milk into the flour mixture a little at a time, whisking constantly to keep the mixture smooth and lump-free. Return to the heat and cook gently, still stirring, until the sauce becomes thick and creamy.

Remove from the heat and leave to cool. Stir

in the whisked eggs, the grated cheese and the nutmeg. Taste and adjust the seasoning with salt and pepper as required.

You are now ready to assemble your moussaka.

Remove the cinnamon sticks from the meat sauce.

Take a good sized, deep-sided baking dish and begin by spreading a little of the meat sauce over the bottom.

On top of this lay the aubergine slices so they overlap each other. Sprinkle with half of the grated cheese and pour meat sauce evenly over the aubergines and continue in this order until all the ingredients have been used finishing with the meat sauce on top.

Carefully pour the béchamel sauce over everything so that it is completely covered, sprinkle with a little nutmeg and bake for 1 hour.

After cooking, leave the moussaka for at least one hour to rest and allow to cool before serving. A crisp, green salad works very well as an accompaniment to this rich dish.

TIP: *Pecorino cheese is ideal, but any strong cheese will do*

*T*his recipe originates from the neighbouring island of Kefalonia, and the secret to its success is in mixing the meats. It will not taste the same if you use all beef or all lamb. If you want to be really extravagant, you can replace 250g of the beef mince with chicken and make the filling with three meats. This is a rich pie, and a little goes a long way. Best served warm (rather than piping hot straight from the oven) it needs nothing more than a crisp green salad to accompany it as a main dish or serve in smaller pieces for a party buffet.

serves 6

1 450g packet of filo pastry
500g of lean minced beef
250g of lean minced lamb
1 large red onion, finely chopped
3 garlic cloves, crushed
1 glass of red wine
250g tin of chopped tomatoes
1 teaspoon of sweet paprika
1 teaspoon of ground coriander
2 tablespoons of dried thyme
a good handful of fresh, chopped parsley
2 tablespoons of breadcrumbs
1 free-range egg, lightly beaten
100g of grated kefalotiri or pecorino cheese
salt and black pepper
3 tablespoons of olive oil, plus some for brushing the pastry

Heat 3 tablespoons of olive oil in a large saucepan and, when hot, add the onions and sauté gently for 2 to 3 minutes.

Add the garlic and continue to sauté gently for another couple of minutes.

Add the minced meats and cook, breaking up with a wooden spoon to prevent any lumps forming. When the meat juices are absorbed and the meats are crumbly add the wine, tomatoes with their juices, paprika, coriander and thyme. Season generously with salt and pepper and cook for 40 minutes until all the liquids have been absorbed.

Remove from the heat and let the mixture cool down before adding the parsley, the cheese, the breadcrumbs and the egg. Mix these in very well.

Heat the oven to 180C

While this mixture is cooling, open your filo pastry and brush each sheet individually with olive oil.

Lay half of the pastry sheets in a greased pie dish to make the bottom of your pie. Put the meat mixture in and lay the rest of the filo on top.

Brush the top again with olive oil, fold the excess top and bottom sheets of filo together to make your pie and sprinkle with water.

Using a sharp knife, mark out portions by carefully slitting through the top layers of the filo.

Bake for 45 to 50 minutes until the pastry is golden.

*T*his is a great recipe that impresses at every barbecue. The children (not to mention the adults) love it and have great fun making their own bifteki parcels by spreading a little tsatsiki over their pitta bread, putting some salad on top, and laying a bifteki (or in my case two) on that, sprinkling with a few chips and then folding the edges of the pitta in and rolling the bottom up, rather like a wrap.

If this all sounds too messy and hands-on for you, it is just as delicious served on a plate… as so many of my customers at the taverna can vouch for.

serves 4

800g of minced beef

1 large red onion, finely chopped

3 cloves of garlic, finely chopped

4 tablespoons of dried breadcrumbs

1 tablespoon of dried oregano

1 tablespoon of dried mint

1 bunch of fresh parsley, finely chopped

1 teaspoon ground cumin

2 teaspoons of salt

half a teaspoon of black pepper

2 to 3 tablespoons of olive oil

1 free-range egg, lightly beaten

for the baste

3 tablespoons of olive oil

I teaspoon of good mustard

juice of 1 lemon

a little freshly ground black pepper

If you have a food processor, put in all the ingredients except the minced meat and the egg, and whizz for 1 minute so they are all extremely finely chopped. If you don't have a food processor then the best way to get the onion and garlic fine enough for this recipe is to grate them, and chop the herbs as fine as you possibly can.

Put the mincemeat in a large bowl, add the finely chopped mixture, pour in the egg, and then knead everything together to blend thoroughly until you have a nice, firm consistency.

Cover the bowl with cling-film and put in the refrigerator for at least half an hour, or until you are ready to use it.

Take the mixture and make pattie-shaped meatballs with it. These can be either put under the grill or barbecued (you can also bake them in a moderate oven).

Put the baste ingredients in a shallow bowl and whisk well until the mixture thickens. Baste the meatballs before and during cooking.

TIP: *Serve on warm pitta bread with tzatziki (see page 37), a mixed salad and home-made fries*

This dish not only tastes fabulous, but looks impressive too. It's a little fiddly to assemble, but so worth the effort. It has been one of our highly successful specials at The Olive Tree for many years now... in fact, we have three generations of a family who visit us regularly and always place a special order for it as soon as they arrive.

serves 4

4 medium size aubergines, cut in half length wise (keep the stems on)
300g of lean minced beef
2 good sized onions, finely chopped
3 garlic cloves, crushed
1 glass of red wine
1 cinnamon stick
a large handful of mixed, chopped fresh

basil, parsley and mint
olive oil
salt and freshly ground black pepper
1 ripe large tomato, chopped
1 tablespoon tomato puree
500g approx of mashed potato
50g grated pecorino (or parmesan) cheese
a sprinkle of ground nutmeg

Halve the aubergines lengthwise, leaving the stems intact. Take a metal spoon and scrape out some flesh from each aubergine half to leave a hollow. Reserve the scooped out flesh.

Put the aubergine shells into a colander and sprinkle lightly with salt to draw out any bitter juices.

After about 15-20 minutes, rinse the aubergine shells in water and dry well.

Meanwhile, put potatoes on to boil. Heat 2 to 3 tablespoons of olive oil in a saucepan and fry onions and garlic for 5 minutes until soft.

Add the minced meat and fry, stirring frequently, until all the meat juices are absorbed and the meat is crumbly.

Finely chop the reserved aubergine flesh and add it to the meat, together with the red wine, chopped tomatoes, tomato puree and cinnamon stick.

Season generously with salt and pepper and simmer, uncovered, for 20 minutes, then add the fresh herbs into the mix and simmer for a further 2 minutes.

If the sauce looks to be drying out too much during cooking time, add a very small amount of water, but only if needed. The finished consistency should be nice and thick, for your filling.

Now heat the oven to 200C

Brush the drained, dried aubergine shells with olive oil and place under the grill for a few minutes (skin side down) until they turn light golden. They absorb quite a lot of oil, so keep them basted and don't allow them to dry out.

Place the aubergine shells into a lightly oiled, shallow, baking dish and spoon the minced meat mixture into the hollows.

Sprinkle with half of the grated cheese and cover with the mashed potato.

Sprinkle the potato with the ground nutmeg and the rest of the cheese and bake for 40 minutes, or until the potato topping has turned a golden brown.

In essence, this is the Greek equivalent of the Italian lasagne. As well as being a delicious but relatively inexpensive way to feed a large, hungry family as a main meal, it is also a very popular Greek party dish, served in small squares as part of a buffet. My dad loved pastitsio the way his mum made it when he was a child... with the fattest, longest bucatini you can find. He told us it filled you up better as the pasta was hollow and you ended up sucking in as much air as pasta, while you struggled to get a forkful into your mouth without it all unravelling and falling back onto the plate. I recommend using rigatoni or penne to avoid this experience.

serves 6-8

500g bucatini (long, hollow pasta – rigatoni or penne also work well if you can't find bucatini)

1 egg, beaten

60g grated kefalotiri cheese – you can use pecorino or parmesan as a substitute

for the béchamel sauce

120g butter

120g plain flour

1 litre of milk

2 eggs, beaten

half a teaspoon of ground nutmeg

half of the cheese (30g)

for the meat sauce

1kg lean minced beef

1 large onion, finely chopped

3-4 garlic cloves, finely chopped

2 cinnamon sticks

1 glass red wine

2 bay leaves

a pinch of cloves

400g tin of chopped tomatoes

1 tablespoon of tomato puree

1 tablespoon of dried oregano

salt and pepper

4 tablespoons of olive oil

TIP: *Pastitsio requires almost every pot, pan and utensil you have in your kitchen, so allow yourself plenty of time to prepare and cook this dish*

then add the pasta and cook al-dente.

Drain well and transfer to a lightly greased baking dish. Leave to cool slightly. Add the one beaten egg and mix well.

For the béchamel sauce, melt the butter in a non-stick saucepan. Add the flour and cook over a medium heat, stirring all the time, for 1 minute.

Gradually beat in the milk, bring to the boil and simmer for 2 to 3 minutes, stirring, until the mixture is thick and creamy.

Remove from the heat and add half of the cheese (30g), the two beaten eggs and stir briskly. Season with salt, pepper and nutmeg and mix well.

To assemble your Pastitsio

Take 3 to 4 tablespoons of the béchamel sauce and a quarter of the minced meat sauce and pour these over the pasta in your baking dish. Mix everything well.

Spread the pasta to cover the base of the dish, pour in the rest of the meat sauce, spreading it all on top of the pasta.

Pour the béchamel sauce over the top and shake your dish from side to side to allow the sauce to cover all of the meat and pasta. Sprinkle with the rest of the cheese and a little more nutmeg.

Bake for 40 to 45 minutes until golden brown.

Heat the olive oil in a large saucepan and, when hot, add the chopped onions and garlic and cook until golden. Add the cinnamon sticks and minced meat and cook, stirring all the time, until the mince is brown and crumbly.

Pour in the wine and the tomatoes. Add the tomato puree, bay leaves and cloves, then season to taste with salt and pepper. Simmer uncovered for 30-40 minutes, or until the sauce has thickened.

Add the oregano, stir well to mix and remove from the heat.

At this point heat the oven to 180C.

Meanwhile, bring approximately 4 litres of water to the boil in a large saucepan.

When it begins to boil add 1 teaspoon of salt,

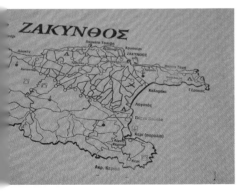

Lamb

Arni

A butcher in Zakynthos town, 1986

*A*n all-time favourite in our family, especially in spring-time when the lamb is sweet and the artichokes are plentiful. The combination of the sweetness of the lamb, the sharpness of the lemon and the slightly bitter artichokes works so well, all brought perfectly together with the egg and lemon sauce. This was one of my mum's best dishes and we would have it often on a Sunday as children… I'm ashamed to say that I used to pick the artichokes out back then, but now I adore them.

serves 4

1kg of shoulder of lamb cut into portions with the bone left in

1 tablespoon of plain flour

salt and black pepper

3 tablespoons of olive oil

4 spring onions, finely chopped

1 tablespoon of fresh dill, finely chopped

2 tablespoons of fresh parsley, chopped

juice of 1 lemon

half a pint of hot vegetable stock

12 globe artichoke hearts

for the fricassée sauce

3 egg yolks and the juice from another lemon.

Season the flour with salt and black pepper and toss the lamb pieces in it until well coated, shaking off any excess flour.

Heat the olive oil in a heavy-bottomed flameproof cooking pan and, when hot, add the lamb pieces and sauté until evenly browned. Add the spring onions and cook for 2 more minutes, then add the parsley, dill and lemon juice.

Cover the meat with the stock, put the lid on and simmer over a medium heat for 90 minutes, stirring occasionally so that it doesn't stick.

Add the artichoke hearts and cook for a further 30 minutes or until the lamb is tender and the artichokes are soft. Remove from the heat and make the fricasse sauce.

Put 4 to 5 tablespoons of the lamb juices into a bowl and leave to cool slightly before adding the egg yolks and lemon juice. Beat this mixture with a fork as if you were whisking an omelette. When it is nice and frothy, pour it back into the cooking pan over the meat, shake the pan so that the egg and lemon mixture gets incorporated.

Leave to rest for 5 minutes before serving.

This is such a simple but delicious way to cook lamb and the secret is the herbs. Use the most aromatic oregano and thyme that you can find.

Here on Zakynthos we have some of the best in Greece, growing wild up in the mountainous northern region of the island. The mother of our son's godfather is from this area and presented us with a couple of roots of each herb as gifts when we had finished building our house. Our garden in Kypseli is quite stony and the herbs have thrived here, so we are lucky...we only have to go into the garden to pick them.

We dry the oregano once a year and Diana collects great armfuls of it and hangs it to dry in our kitchen...the whole house smells wonderful. Once dried, it is rubbed fine, twigs removed, put into airtight jars and into the store cupboard for use at home and at the taverna. We find the thyme is much better used fresh and we simply pick this as and when we need it.

serves 4

1 shoulder of lamb, cut into portions with the bone left in
8 garlic cloves, unpeeled
2 tablespoons of dried oregano
3 to 4 sprigs fresh thyme
3 tablespoons of olive oil
juice and zest from 1 lemon
salt and freshly ground black pepper

Heat oven to 200C

Place the lamb portions, olive oil, lemon juice, zest, and herbs into a large bowl. Season generously with salt and black pepper and mix everything together well with your hands.

Break the cloves of garlic off the head but don't peel them. Mix them into the meat, skins on.

Cut a large piece of greaseproof paper and a bigger one of foil, both big enough to wrap the meat in.

Place the meat on the greaseproof paper and wrap it into a large parcel, then wrap this tightly in the foil so that your parcel won't leak any of the precious cooking juices during baking.

Place the parcel in a baking dish, pour a glass of water around it and bake for 2 hours, checking regularly and sparingly topping up the water as needed. just so it doesn't burn.

Take the parcel out, remove the paper and foil, return the meat to the dish and bake for another 30 minutes on a high heat to give the meat a lovely colour.

Youvetsi is a very old, traditional Greek recipe that has been enjoyed for generations.

The name derives from the clay pot that was originally used to cook it in, over an open fire.

It is one of my personal favourites and will always evoke memories of family gatherings and celebrations over the years.

Because it's cooked in the meat juices, the pasta is the tastiest you'll ever have and, as a one-pot meal, there's minimal washing up.

serves 4

600-700g of lean lamb off the bone, and cut into cubes

1 large red onion, finely chopped

4 cloves garlic, crushed

2 bay leaves

1 cinnamon stick

a pinch of cloves

250ml dry red wine

Heat the olive oil in a large saucepan. When hot add the chopped onion and fry for 2 minutes. Add the crushed garlic and cook for a further 2 minutes, then add the lamb, spices, bay leaves and red wine. Cover and simmer slowly for 1 hour.

Add the chopped tomatoes and the tomato puree to the pot, season with salt and pepper and stir well. Simmer for another hour, or until the lamb is tender.

Turn the heat off. Remove the meat with a slotted spoon and put into a large serving dish together with some of the sauce from the pan and keep warm.

Add about three-quarters of the hot stock to the saucepan with the remaining meat juices and place back on the heat and bring to the boil, then add the kritharaki pasta and simmer slowly until the pasta is cooked and the juices are absorbed, stirring continuously to prevent it from sticking to the bottom of the pan.

If you need to, gradually add as much of the stock as required – if you need to add more, add small amounts of hot water during this process so that the pasta has enough to cook in, but does not need draining when it's cooked.

Pour the hot pasta over the meat, mix well and sprinkle with plenty of grated kefalotiri or pecorino cheese to taste.

400g tin of chopped tomatoes
1 tablespoon of tomato puree
salt and a generous amount of black pepper
4 tablespoons of olive oil
1 pint of hot vegetable stock
250g of kritharaki pasta (also known as orzo or risono)
150g of kefalotiri or pecorino cheese, grated

TIP: *Lamb would be the traditional choice of meat for this dish, but it also works extremely well with beef and even chicken. If you choose to use either of these, the method remains the same, but you will have to adjust the cooking time accordingly.*

A legendary dish that has been adapted and modified over the generations so that there are now as many versions of the dish as there are cooks preparing it. The name *kleftiko* means stolen and the recipe was originally invented out of necessity by the partisans who were fighting the occupation of our country centuries ago. They were living and fighting in the hills and mountains, so a stolen lamb now and then was more than welcome.

Having acquired their animal, they would dig a deep hole in the ground, fill it with hot charcoals, put their meat and mountain herbs in and then cover it and leave it to cook for many hours. This way there was very little risk of giving their position away… as opposed to setting a fire and letting the enemy know exactly where they were by the smoke and heavenly smells wafting through the air. These days we don't dig holes of course, but to honour the history of the dish my mum taught me to keep the ingredients as authentic as possible… if it was good enough for the partisans, then it's good enough for us. I totally agree with her, and so have more than 30 years' worth of Olive Tree customers who come back time after time for this wonderful dish.

serves 6

1 leg of lamb (about 1.5k-2 kg), bone in and cut into serving portions (ask your butcher to do this for you)

4 large cloves of garlic, finely chopped

2 glasses of dry red wine

2 bay leaves

1 sprig fresh thyme, chopped

1 sprig fresh rosemary, chopped

1 cup of fresh parsley, chopped

salt and freshly ground black pepper

200ml of vegetable or chicken stock

3 tablespoons of olive oil

TIP: *The traditional cut for this dish is a whole shoulder, a full of flavour but fattier bonier piece of meat, which we Greeks prefer. I use leg in the restaurant to cater for more refined palates, but both work equally well. It's up to you. Either of them can be cut by your butcher into individual portions to make serving easier, but they must have the bone in if you are going to cook an authentic kleftiko.*

Heat the oven to 200C

While the oven is pre-heating, heat the olive oil in a large frying pan and brown the lamb pieces evenly.

You might have to do this in batches, depending on the size of your frying pan, but make sure you don't overcrowd the pan or the meat won't brown nicely.

Put the browned meat into a large earthenware cooking pot or deep casserole dish.

In the same oil, fry the chopped garlic for 1 minute and then add the red wine. Simmer for 1 more minute, then pour over the meat in the cooking pot.

Add all the rest of the ingredients and stir to mix well. Cover tightly... if your pot hasn't got a lid use a layer of greaseproof paper covered with a layer of foil as a makeshift lid and cook for 2 hours and 30 minutes. Check the meat... it should be tender and ready to fall off the bone.

If needed, leave to cook for a little longer. until the lamb is tender.

Beef

Moschari

Sofrito is native to the island of Corfu, where I grew up.

If you love garlic, and you must love garlic to enjoy a proper sofrito, you will be in for an absolute treat with this dish. The authentic Corfiot way to serve it is with mashed potato…a perfect accompaniment for the gloriously thick, delicious sauce and tender beef.

This is without doubt our all-time, best-selling meat dish at The Olive Tree… and justifiably so.

serves 4

700g very lean beef cut into thin slices

2 whole garlic heads peeled and grated – of course you can reduce the amount to your taste

5 tablespoons of olive oil,

4 tablespoons of plain flour

salt and black pepper

plenty of fresh parsley, finely chopped

1 sprig fresh thyme

2 tablespoons of white wine vinegar

a glass of white wine

500ml of hot beef stock

Season the flour well with the salt and pepper and toss the beef slices in this to coat. Shake off any excess flour.

Heat the olive oil in a large frying pan and when the oil starts smoking fry the beef slices for about 1 minute on each side, to seal and colour. Take care not to overcrowd the pan and cook the beef in batches if necessary.

Place the sealed beef in a large, heavy-

bottomed flameproof cooking pot.

Using the same oil in the frying pan, add the grated garlic and chopped parsley and fry for 2 to 3 minutes, stirring.

Add all the liquids to the frying pan (the vinegar, wine and stock) and simmer for 2 minutes, stirring and scraping the bottom of the pan to get any meat juices mixed in. Pour this over the meat in the cooking pot.

Put the thyme sprig into the cooking pot,

check the seasoning and add more black pepper to taste. Mix well, cover and simmer for 1 hour 30 minutes or until the meat is tender.

You will need to stir this from time to time to keep the flour from sticking. This should give you plenty of beautiful thick, rich sauce at the end of cooking. Add a little hot water if your sauce looks too thick or dry while you are cooking the dish.

*L*emonato is a popular dish and is often on the table for Greek Sunday lunch. The recipe is extremely versatile and you can adapt it for other meats by simply altering the herbs. When we cook lemonato with lamb we use rosemary instead of the thyme and celery replaces it if we use pork.

serves 4

600g of lean stewing beef cut into 2cm slices (in the Olive Tree we use rump steak)

4 garlic cloves, whole

2 sprigs of fresh thyme

1 tablespoon of dried oregano

4-5 tablespoons of olive oil

300ml of hot vegetable stock

black pepper

juice and zest from 1 unwaxed lemon

Heat the olive oil in a large heavy-based flameproof cooking pot and, when hot, add the meat and brown the slices evenly.

Add the garlic and sauté for 2 more minutes before adding the herbs, pepper and stock

You won't need salt because of the stock cube.

Cover with the lid and simmer for 1 hour and 45 minutes or until the meat is tender, checking throughout the cooking period that there are enough juices in the pan. Add a little hot water if necessary.

Add the lemon juice and zest and continue to simmer gently for another 15 minutes.

*P*robably the most famous Greek casserole dish and a firm
favourite on our menu at The Olive Tree. Stifado was
originally made with rabbit or hare, but with more and more
of the population living in cities and game not being readily
available, the recipe has been adapted over the generations and
is now usually made with beef. If you can get hold of a rabbit…or
even better, a hare, the cooking method is exactly the same, but the
cooking times will need to be adjusted.

serves 4

700g lean stewing beef, cubed

1 large onion finely chopped

3 garlic cloves crushed

2 cinnamon sticks

1 glass of red wine

salt and black pepper

about 100ml of hot water

250g tin of crushed tomatoes

1 tablespoon of tomato puree

1 teaspoon of sugar

2 bay leaves

half a teaspoon of ground allspice

a pinch of ground cloves
20 shallots

Heat the olive oil in a large heavy-based flameproof cooking pot and, when hot, add the meat and fry until nicely browned all over.

Add the onion, garlic and cinnamon sticks and simmer for a few more minutes.

Add the wine and cook for 2 minutes. Season with salt and pepper and add enough hot water to cover the meat. Put the lid on and simmer for 1 hour.

While this is simmering away, prepare the shallots. Peel them and slit a cross on the bottom with a sharp knife.

Bring a small pan of water to the boil and blanche the shallots for 2 minutes. Drain and keep aside.

After the casserole has been cooking for 1 hour, add the crushed tomatoes, tomato puree, bay leaves, allspice and ground cloves and simmer for a further 30 minutes.

Add the shallots to the casserole and cook for another 15 minutes until both they and the meat are soft and tender.

*M*y mum's dad was a butcher so, despite the war, meat was always plentiful in their house as she was growing up in the Peloponnese. This is a third generation recipe which my mum learned from her mother, and taught me.

The secret is to allow the beef to cook in it's own juices in the initial stages of cooking. This intensifies and concentrates the flavour. The resulting gravy makes this an absolutely delicious way to roast beef.

serves 4

600-700g lean beef, cubed

1 large onion, finely chopped

3 garlic cloves, finely chopped

1 carrot, grated

1 celery stalk, finely chopped

a generously large handful of fresh parsley, finely chopped

a handful of fresh dill, chopped

juice and zest from 1 unwaxed lemon

salt and black pepper

1 tablespoon of dried thyme or oregano

5 tablespoons of olive oil

1 tablespoon of flour

Heat the olive oil in a large, heavy-based cooking pot and, when hot, brown the meat evenly. Add the chopped onions and garlic and fry together with the meat for a further 2 minutes. Add the carrot, celery and herbs and sauté everything together for another 3 to 4 minutes.

Add the flour and cook, stirring continuously for 1 more minute before adding the lemon juice, zest, salt, pepper and enough hot water to just cover the meat. Simmer gently for about 1 hour and 30 minutes or until the beef is tender.

My favourite accompaniment to this dish is pasta cooked in the meat juices. When the dish is ready place the meat and half of the meat juices (the sauce) in another dish and keep warm. Add 1 pint of hot water to the cooking pot and a little salt, bring to boil and add the pasta , any pasta is lovely, I prefer spaghetti or penne.

Serve the hot pasta on a plate add the beef on top and sprinkle some pecorino or parmesan.

*T*his dish takes it's name from the pot it is cooked in. A Stamna is a clay or earthenware stewing pot with a tight fitting lid for oven cooking. A good oven dish with a lid is a perfectly acceptable substitute.

In the spring of 1983 Diana and I went for a short break to the tiny Cyclades island of Sifnos, and we stayed in a small room down at the sleepy little harbour there.

Early every morning we would take one of the two island buses and ride up the hill to the island's capital town of Apollonia, about 15 minutes away, for a coffee and decide what to do with our day. We would share the rickety old bus with a few locals, plenty of chickens, the odd goat or lamb and lots of stamnas, all brightly painted with their owners' names on the side. The bus-driver, called Apostolis, would take the stamnas to the local bakery up in Apollonia where they would be baked in the residual heat of the huge ovens (the day's bread having been baked already).

Apostolis' favour didn't end there though. Once the stamnas were cooked, he would meander through the countryside delivering them to the farmers working in their fields, together with any livestock that was meant for them too.

It was our most favourite way to wile away the morning, chugging along on this bus with no particular set route at all, enveloped in the rich, mouthwatering aromas of the stamnas that would make our stomachs rumble.

Of course, Apostolis knew all of the farmers and where their land was and every day the route would be different, depending on who's wife had prepared what, so we got to see a lot of the island. The bus would shudder to a halt, he'd honk his horn and yell the farmer's name out of the window. Within minutes the farmer's lad would come running up to the roadside to collect the delicious pot of wonderful meat stew for lunch. Now that's service for you!

serves 4

600 to 700g of stewing beef

1 red onion, chopped

2 garlic cloves, chopped

1 celery stalk, chopped

1 carrot, chopped

A good handful of mixed fresh thyme, fresh parsley , fresh chopped rosemary

1 glass of dry white wine

3 tablespoons of olive oil

salt and black pepper

half a pint of vegetable stock

If you have a clay or earthenware cooking pot for this dish then put the meat and all the other ingredients, except the stock, directly into it. If not, simply do the same but in a large non-permeable bowl. Mix well and put the lid on, or cover with cling film. Leave to marinate in the fridge, ideally overnight, if you have the time, otherwise marinate for a minimum of 2 hours.

Now-heat oven to 180C.

If your meat has been marinating overnight in the fridge, take it out for 30 minutes to come to room temperature before cooking. Pour the stock over the meat and put the stew pot into the oven to bake slowly for 2 hours 30 minutes, until the meat is tender.

*T*his is my twist on the ever-popular classic Italian dish. Whenever I cook it at the taverna I can never cook enough. The resulting rich gravy the beef produces is just divine and we usually serve the dish accompanied by mashed potato...the perfect partnership. When we cook this at home, our favourite cut to use is oxtail. If you can manage to get hold of one, try it for yourselves... you won't be disappointed.

Be prepared, though, you'll need plenty of moistened hand towels, because it's impossible to take all the beautiful meat off the tail without using your fingers – It's deliciously messy.

serves 4

4 pieces of oxtail or shin on the bone, about 300g each

4 tablespoons of olive oil

2 tablespoons of plain flour, seasoned with salt and black pepper

1 red onion, finely chopped

3 garlic cloves, finely chopped

2 glasses of good red wine

1 pint of chicken stock

250g of freshly chopped tomatoes

1 sprig of fresh rosemary

1 sprig of fresh thyme

A handful of fresh parsley, chopped

1 tablespoon of fresh basil, chopped (or 2 teaspoons of dried basil if you can't find fresh)

1 tablespoon of dried oregano

Toss the beef pieces in the seasoned flour, shaking off any excess. Heat the olive oil in a large frying pan and, when hot, brown the beef all over for a few minutes. You might need to do this in batches, depending on the size of your frying pan. When the beef is browned, take it from the pan and put it in a large, heavy-bottomed saucepan or saute pan.

Using the same oil you browned the beef in, gently fry the chopped onion and garlic until golden.

Add all the herbs except the oregano and cook gently for 2 more minutes before adding the wine, the tomatoes and the stock.

Bring to the boil and pour into the casserole pan, making sure the beef pieces are covered with the stock mixture. Add a little hot water if necessary to cover the beef. Taste and adjust seasoning if needed. Put the lid on the casserole and simmer gently for 3 hours, or until the meat is tender.

About 5 minutes before the end of cooking, sprinkle with the oregano and stir through.

TIP: *For more gracious dining, I use shin beef in the taverna. It gives the same rich-tasting result and is far easier to tackle with cutlery*

Other meat dishes

Alla piata me kreata

I invented this easy and delicious recipe in 1981 when I first met Diana who had come to work in my Dad's taverna in Corfu.

Me and my brother Vangelis used to do Greek dancing every night, creating a great atmosphere and keeping the tourists entertained until the early hours... Diana was kept very busy serving them.

I wanted to impress her so, one particularly busy night, I disappeared into the kitchen at around 3am to cook us something special.

By the time we had seen the last customers off the premises, cleared up the bar, restocked the fridges and locked the doors, the steaks were ready and I could begin my flirting... my plan must have worked, because we're still together.

serves 4

4 pork steaks

a few potatoes, peeled and cut into thick wedges

a sprig of rosemary

a sprig of thyme

2 garlic cloves, finely sliced

4 tablespoons of olive oil

half a pint of hot chicken stock

1 glass of good red wine

a little salt and plenty of black pepper

Heat the olive oil in a large frying pan and, when hot, fry the pork steaks for couple of minutes on each side until nicely browned. If they don't all fit in, then fry them two at a time so that they will colour properly.

Remove the steaks and place them in a wide, flameproof cooking pot large enough to hold them all.

In the same oil fry the potato wedges, turning them until nice and golden all over.

Take them from the frying pan with a slotted spoon and put them in the cooking pot together with the pork chops.

Add the sliced garlic and the sprigs of thyme and rosemary to the frying pan and cook gently for a couple of minutes.

Add the wine and stock to the frying pan, bring to boil stirring to scrape any meat juices off the bottom and pour over the pork steaks and potatoes in the cooking pot.

Season well with pepper and add a little salt if needed – the stock may have been salty enough that you might not need any, so taste first.

Put the cooking pot over a gentle heat and simmer slowly for 45 minutes or until the meat and potatoes are nice and tender.

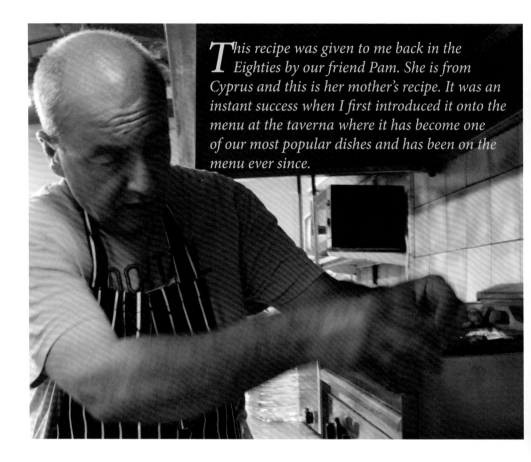

This recipe was given to me back in the Eighties by our friend Pam. She is from Cyprus and this is her mother's recipe. It was an instant success when I first introduced it onto the menu at the taverna where it has become one of our most popular dishes and has been on the menu ever since.

serves 4

1kg of lean pork, cut in to slices
1 teaspoon of ground coriander
3 bay leaves
1 red onion, finely chopped
4-5 tablespoons of olive oil
12 baby new potatoes

500ml of good dry red wine
1 vegetable stock cube
1 teaspoon of sweet paprika
2 sprigs of fresh thyme
salt and black pepper
a handful of fresh finely chopped parsley

Place the pork, coriander and bay leaves in a large non-porous bowl. Pour in the wine, mix well, cover with cling film and leave to marinate, preferably overnight in the fridge.

Lift the pork out of the bowl with a slotted spoon, reserving the marinade for later use in the recipe. Dry the pork with kitchen paper.

Heat the olive oil in a large frying pan and cook the onions for 3 to 4 minutes until soft and golden.

Remove the onions with a slotted spoon and put into a wide, shallow, fireproof casserole pan or saucepan.

In the same oil brown the potatoes quickly, turning them until they are golden. At this point you are not cooking the potatoes, simply giving them a good colour.

Remove with a slotted spoon and place them into your pan with the onions. In the oil left in the frying pan, sauté the pork pieces for 2 minutes on each side until nicely coloured.

Pour the reserved marinade over the pork in the frying pan, crumble the stock cube, then stir well, scraping the base of the pan to get any caramelised meat juices mixed in as well. Bring to the boil, cover and simmer slowly for 20 minutes.

Pour the meat mixture over the potatoes and onions in your casserole pan.

Add the paprika, thyme, black pepper and salt to taste, stir a couple of times, cover and simmer very slowly for 1 hour.

Finally sprinkle in the fresh parsley, remove from the heat and leave your pork to rest for 10 minutes before serving.

*W*hen my mum was a child, she had two elder cousins who were hunters.

She remembered them being away for days at a time and coming back on their horses, laden with game they had shot, which her father would buy for his butcher's shop.

Wild hare or rabbit were plentiful in those days and this is the recipe my mum remembered helping her mother prepare and cook.

Rabbit is easily available in butchers today and is a very healthy and economical choice of meat… not to mention extremely delicious too. Our family have always eaten this dish with pasta (usually penne), sprinkled with grated kefalotiri or pecorino and accompanied by a carafe of good red wine.

serves 4

for soaking overnight

1 medium size hare or rabbit cut into serving pieces

A bowl of cold water

3 to 4 tablespoons of vinegar

1 large onion, cut in quarters

to cook

4-5 tablespoons of olive oil

1 small red onion, finely chopped

6 spring onions, finely chopped

a good handful of fresh dill and parsley, finely chopped

2 sprigs of fresh thyme

1 celery stalk, finely chopped

half of a carrot, grated

salt and pepper

200ml of hot chicken stock

1 glass of white wine

1 knob of butter

Put the hare or rabbit pieces in a bowl with enough cold water to cover the meat. Stir in the vinegar and add the quartered onion. Cover with cling film and put into the fridge overnight. Don't be tempted to skip this soaking process as it removes the heavy game smell from the meat and sweetens it.

The following day, drain the meat pieces well and dry with kitchen paper.

Heat the oil in a heavy-bottomed flameproof casserole pan and, when hot, fry the meat pieces on all sides until golden brown, add the chopped onions and cook for 3 more minutes. Add the herbs, celery and carrot, pour in the wine and the stock and stir to mix well. Season with salt, if necessary, and plenty of freshly ground black pepper.

Cover the casserole and simmer for 1 hour 30 minutes until the meat is tender, checking now and again to make sure there is always enough liquid in the pan.

When the meat is cooked, take the pan off the heat. Add the butter and stir through to thicken the sauce.

serves 4

4 spicy country sausages, sliced

1 red onion, roughly chopped

2 cloves of garlic, finely chopped

1 green pepper, roughly chopped

1 red pepper, roughly chopped

1 yellow pepper, roughly chopped

1 tin of chopped tomatoes

1 tablespoon of tomato puree

A mug of water

4 to 5 tablespoons of olive oil

A glass of red wine

1 teaspoon of sugar

1 bay leaf

2 chilli peppers (optional)

A pinch of paprika

Sea salt and freshly ground pepper

Add 1 tablespoon of olive oil to a saucepan over high heat and sauté the sausages. When nicely coloured remove with a slotted spoon and put aside on some kitchen paper to drain.

Into the same pan, add the rest of the olive oil and the onion, season with freshly ground pepper and cook for one minute. Then add the garlic and tomato puree and cook for another minute. Add peppers and continue to cook for a further two minutes.

Deglaze the pan with red wine, taking care not to be splashed as it sizzles. Scrape any bits left on the bottom and cook gently until the wine evaporates. Then add the sugar, canned tomatoes, a cup of water, the bay leaf and spices, turn the heat down to medium and cook for 25 to 30 minutes with the lid on, until the peppers soften.

Add the sausages and cook a little longer with the lid off until the sauce thickens. Check seasoning and adjust if necessary.

Allow to cool a little before serving with crusty bread.

TIP: *You can find spicy Greek sausages in a delicatessen or Mediterranean supermarkets*

Sweet things

Epidorpia

This is the perfect end to a rich meal. Unlike some rice puddings it is light and creamy with a subtle flavour of lemon and cinnamon running through.

Put the rice in a pan with 300ml of water and simmer over a low heat for 8 to 10 minutes until most of the water has been absorbed.

Keep 2 tablespoons of the milk and add the rest into the pan with lemon zest and continue to simmer for another 20 minutes stirring now and then until the mixture becomes thick and creamy.

Mix the cornflour with the remaining milk and add it to the rice together with the sugar and simmer for another 3 minutes.

Remove from heat and leave to cool slightly.

Lightly beat the egg yolks, add them to the rice and return to the heat and cook gently for 30 seconds until thickened. DO NOT get it too hot or the eggs will scramble.

Spoon the mixture immediately into 4 small shallow bowls, sprinkle with cinnamon and leave to cool.

Serve at room temperature.

serves 4

150g pudding rice
600g full cream fresh milk
finely grated zest from half a lemon
2 teaspoons of cornflour
75g caster sugar
2 egg yolks
ground cinnamon

A classic standard in every Greek household. I remember my grandmother making these and the way the whole of her little house used be scented with them cooking. The eggs from her free-range hens always made sure the custards were a fabulous deep yellow-orange colour, so try to get the best eggs you can for this simple, delightful dessert.

serves 4

6 egg yolks
75g caster sugar
450ml Greek yoghurt
ground cinnamon

Beat the egg yolks and sugar until pale and creamy.

Gradually beat in the yoghurt and continue beating until the mixture is smooth.

Pour the mixture into 4 individual soufflé dishes or ramekins and sprinkle every one of them generously with cinnamon.

Stand the dishes in a roasting pan with water to come half-way up the dishes.

Bake in the oven at 180C, 350F or gas mark 4 for 30 minutes until set.

Remove from the oven and stand on a wire rack to cool.

Serve chilled with fresh fruit.

serves 4 - 6

400g apricots stoned and cut in half
2 tablespoons of Greek honey
2 tablespoons of rose water
juice from half of a lemon
400g Greek yoghurt
1 cup crushed pistachio nuts
few mint leaves to decorate

Put apricots, rose water, honey and lemon juice in a blender and pulse until they are a smooth puree.
Divide the puree into individual glasses cover with yoghurt. Sprinkle pistachios and garnish with couple of mint leaves.

Refrigerate for at least 2 hours.

TIP: *This can be preprared a day before you want to use it so long as you keep it in the fridge, but don't add the yoghurt until just before it is served.*

*P*robably the best known of all Greek desserts, Baklava is actually a pastry, and a Greek would normally eat it with a little cup of strong coffee sometime in the afternoon, having enjoyed his siesta. However, served with a scoop of vanilla ice cream, it is one of the most popular desserts we have on our menu.

10 servings

20 sheets of filo pastry cut in half

400g melted butter, unsalted

for the filling

4 tablespoons of honey

2 tablespoons of lemon juice

50g sugar

2 teaspoons of ground cinnamon

1 teaspoon of grated lemon rind

225g almonds toasted 10 minutes in the oven

225g walnuts, chopped

for the syrup

350g sugar

125g honey

600ml water

1 cinnamon stick and a strip of thinly pared lemon rind

For this quantity you will need a baking tin of 33 x 23 cm (13x9in).

Heat the oven to 160C.

Start by combining all the ingredients for the filling in the bowl.

Open a packet of filo and cut the sheets in half. It's important to make sure any filo you're not working with is covered with a clean, damp tea towel or it will dry out and you won't be able to use it.

Brush the baking tin with melted butter and line with 10 sheets of the cut pastry, taking care to also brush each sheet liberally with melted butter.

Sprinkle a third of the filling mixture over the filo, then repeat the process – another 10 sheets of buttered filo, topped with another third of the mixture. Then repeat once more. Cover with the remaining filo sheets, again individually buttered. Trim any excess pastry to about 2cm and fold this over to form an edge. Pour any remaining melted butter over the top and with a sharp knife cut the baklava into diamond shapes, going about halfway though. Bake for 1 hour 30 minutes.

About 15 minutes before the baklava is ready to come out of the oven, make your syrup. Place all the ingredients in a saucepan and stir over a low heat until the honey and the sugar have dissolved. Increase the heat then, and bring to the boil. Boil for 10 minutes, take off the heat and leave to cool slightly. By this time your baklava should be ready to come out of the oven and be left to cool too. You need to pour warm syrup over warm baklava, so that the pastry will soak up all the syrup.

Leave to cool completely and then cut through the scored pastry into portions.

TIP: *Baklava will keep perfectly well out of the fridge for up to 4 days.*

*T*hese little butter and vanilla cookies are made in every household during Easter week, traditionally on Easter Thursday, but will not be eaten until the meal after midnight Mass on Saturday because they contain dairy products. The children enjoy making different shapes with the lovely soft, shiny dough and baking Koulourakia is always a real family affair. We used to make our initials and see whose came out best.

Makes 48

225 g butter, softened
150g caster sugar
1 egg
half a teaspoon vanilla extract
half a teaspoon of almond extract
275g plain flour
1 egg, beaten

Heat the oven to 200 C, gas mark 6.

Grease baking trays or line with greaseproof paper.

In a medium-sized bowl cream together the butter, sugar and egg until smooth. Stir in the vanilla and almond extract. Blend in the flour to form a non-sticky dough and knead by hand to finish.

Take about a teaspoon of dough at a time and hand-roll it into a long sausage, then shape them into twists, s-shapes or wreaths.

Place biscuits 5cm apart on the trays, brush with the beaten egg and then bake for 10 minutes until lightly golden. Cool on a wire rack.

*T*hese buttery little cookies are traditionally baked for Christmas and, like mince pies or Christmas pudding, should be made with love. The secret to them is in the creaming of the butter and sugar and in our house, like many others, this is a joint effort. Everyone participates by congregating round the big table in the kitchen and taking turns at beating the butter vigorously with the sugar, turning it to a pale, almost white colour. Of course, a mixer will do exactly the same job in probably half the time...but that's not the point, or the fun. When the Kourabiethes are made, everyone says 'Kai tou Kronou' to each other which literally translates to 'and again next year' and is a very typical wish that Greeks exchange after happy occasions...like baking Christmas cookies.

Makes 36

225g butter, softened
1 teaspoon of rose water
6 tablespoons of icing sugar
350g of plain flour
80g of chopped walnuts
100g of icing sugar for decoration

*T*IP: *A teaspoon of brandy is commonly used to replace the rosewater as a festive flavouring. You can also substitute walnuts with almonds if preferred.*

Heat the oven to 180 C, gas mark 6.
Grease baking trays or line with greaseproof paper.

In a medium-sized bowl, cream the butter and rosewater until smooth. Combine the six tablespoons of icing sugar and flour and stir into the butter mixture until just blended then add the chopped walnuts and mix well.

You may not need all the flour, but keep adding until you have a fairly stiff dough as it will need to hold its shape during baking.

Pull small pieces of dough, roll them in your hands to make 2.5cm balls and place them on the baking tray and bake for 12 minutes.

Meanwhile, place the remaining icing sugar in a shallow dish or baking tray.

As soon as you can hold them without burning your fingers roll the balls in the icing sugar and put on a cooling rack.

Once cooled roll them in the icing sugar a second time, using a spoon so you don't remove the sugar with your fingers.

They can be stored in an airtight container, surrounded by the remaining sugar.

*E*very Greek household and baker traditionally make these little fried sweet treats to celebrate the region's particular Saint's name day. Every time I catch the tantalising aroma of these honey and cinnamon puffs cooking, I am instantly transported back to my childhood, strolling through the narrow streets of Old Corfu Town after the service to celebrate St Spiridon's Name Day, which is on December 12th. Everyone wears their Sunday best and anyone called Spiros or Spiridula (the feminine version)... which is about 75% of the population of Corfu... will be holding a party in honour of their name and serving platefuls of these warm, little beauties. With the waft of warm honey and cinnamon coming out of every window, I couldn't wait to get home, sit with my family and eat our loukoumades and celebrate too. On Zakynthos we have the same tradition, but we make them on December 17th for St Dionysis' Name Day.

But loukoumades are not confined to name days only. They are a very popular treat, whether home-made and shared by the fireside with family and friends, or in one of the traditional coffee shops called kafeneions and served with a tiny cup of strong, pungent Greek coffee. They would make the perfect sweet to follow an informal barbecue for instance, but are just as versatile at the end of a smart party ...it's your choice.

makes about 30

1 packet (about 15g) of dried yeast
half a teacup of warm water
350g plain flour
half a teaspoon of baking powder
half a teaspoon bicarbonate of soda
half a teaspoon sugar
half a teaspoon salt
one and a half teaspoons ground cinnamon
30ml warm water

1 teaspoon brandy (preferably Metaxa)
vegetable oil for frying

for the syrup
225g good Greek honey
125g sugar
150ml water
A few drops of fresh lemon juice
1 cinnamon stick

Sprinkle the yeast into half a tea-cup of the warm water and stir well. Cover and set aside for about 15 minutes until it becomes frothy.

Meanwhile put the flour into a large bowl and add all the dry ingredients, mixing well.

Add the yeast mixture, the brandy and enough of the warm water to make a thick batter. Mix extremely well to make sure there are no lumps in the batter. Cover with a cloth (or cling film) and leave in a warm place for about 2 hours to double in size.

Towards the end of your batter rising time, prepare the syrup. It needs to be still warm to dip your fritters in before serving, so don't make it too far in advance. Put the syrup ingredients into a saucepan and bring to the boil, stirring. Boil for about 5 minutes until the sugar has dissolved. Keep warm until ready to use.

When your batter has doubled in size, heat oil in a deep-sided frying pan (if you don't have one a saucepan will do the same job)

until it is very hot, but not smoking.

Take two spoons and scoop out a dollop of the batter (about the size of a walnut), drop it into the hot oil and fry until golden brown, turning with a slotted spoon to colour evenly.

Fry batches of the loukoumades like this and drain well on kitchen paper.

Using the slotted spoon, dip them into the syrup, then put them on a serving plate and sprinkle with cinnamon and ground walnuts. Drizzle with a little extra syrup to serve.

TIP: *There are as many variations of loukoumades as there are villages in Greece. The above recipe is the basic, but if you want to experiment, you can either add a flavouring to the flour mix at the beginning, such as vanilla or nutmeg, or add your extra flavouring ingredient, such as raisins or finely grated orange zest, after the batter mixture has risen.*

Serves 4-6

500g of filo pastry

for the filling
4 eggs
65g granulated sugar
200 g full fat Greek yoghurt
125ml sunflower or corn oil
2 knobs of butter
1/2 a teaspoon of vanilla essence
1 teaspoon of baking powder
zest from 2 oranges (keep the juice for the syrup)

for the syrup
100ml fresh orange juice
150ml water
200g white sugar

Put all the filling ingredients, except the orange zest, into a blender. Whizz until the mixture is well blended and smooth. Add the orange zest and whizz for just a couple of seconds more. If you don't have a blender, whisk the eggs in a large bowl by hand, then add the rest of the ingredients (the orange zest can also go in at this point too if you're whisking by hand) and continue whisking until everything is combined.

Now heat the oven to 180C while you assemble the pie. Once out of the packet, remember to keep the filo sheets covered with a clean, damp tea towel until you need them, to save them from drying out.

Brush the baking tin with melted butter and line with half of the filo sheets, each individually brushed with melted butter. Pour the filling mixture on to the pastry and cover

with the rest of the filo, again brushing each sheet with melted butter as you go. There will be excess pastry over the edges of your baking tin, so fold them over and tuck them in to make a neat edge.

Bake for 35 to 40 minutes until the pastry turns a golden colour. Remove from the oven and leave to cool completely to room temperature. While the pie is cooling, make the syrup by putting all the ingredients in a pan over a high heat and bring to the boil. Boil for 5 minutes. Leave for 5 minutes or so to cool slightly, then pour over your cooled pie. The portokalopita must now cool again to room temperature before you can cut it to serve.

Picture by Laura Tams

The team 2013: Marika, Miri, Asadullah, Valentino, Lakis , Diana, Emma, Yanni and Fotini

Another day at the office - 21 dishes cooked in one shift

Index of Recipes

Beef

In lemon sauce 106
Mama Mary's pan-roasted 110
Osso bucco 114
Sofrito 104
Stamna 112
Stifado 108

Chicken

Aromatic casserole 61
Filo pastry pie with cheese and mushroom 70
In Metaxa and cream sauce 64
Oven-fried 72
Pot roasted with sun-dried tomatoes 68
Souvlaki (with bacon) 66
Three pepper and pesto 60
With yoghurt (Yaourtlou) 62
Zoe Louise with lemon and oregano 58

Lamb

Fricassée with artichokes 94
With lemon and herbs 96
Youvetsi 98
Kleftiko 100

Minced meat

Aromatic baked meatballs in yoghurt sauce 76
Meat patties (grilled) 84
Meat pie in filo pastry 82
Moussaka 78
Papoutsakia (Little Shoes) 86
Pastitsio 88

Other meat dishes

Lakis' Pork steaks with potatoes 118
Mama Mary's hare or rabbit casserole 122
Pork afelia 120
Spetsofai 124

Sea food

Baked mackerel with tomatoes and herbs 54
Calamari, deep fried 46
Cod bianco 50
Cod in dry Martini and cream sauce 49
King prawn and bacon souvlaki 52
King prawn saganaki 53
Mussels 47
Skate or cod bourdeto 48

Soup

Chestnut and vegetable 14
Lentil (fakes) 16
Mushroom with pesto 15
Tomato with vermicelli 18

Sweet things

Apricot puree with Greek yoghurt 134
Baked custard 132
Baklava 136
Christmas biscuits (Kourambiedes) 140
Easter biscuits (koulourakia) 138

Honey fritters 142
Orange pie 144
Rice pudding with lemon and cinnamon 130

Vegetable dishes

Artichokes ala polita 34
Baked haloumi and potatoes, thyme and rocket 25
Beetroot, baked with feta and hazelnuts 27
Chickpeas, baked with peppers 31
Courgettes, baked with feta 32
Eggs in fresh tomato sauce 28
Green beans in garlic, lemon and tomato 24
Village salad 23
Lemon roasted potatoes 36
Lentils with lemon and dill 33
Peas and carrots 42
Risotto 26
Skordalia 38
Spicy bourdeto potatoes 30
Spinach and feta pie (Spanakotyropita) 40
Tzatziki 37
Warm potato salad 22

Tsilivi 1986 – Top: The Y-junction on the way to the beach; Middle: The The views from the Olive Tree looking left and right: The team in 1989, Diana with Tassos, Theo and Yiannis